The Growth Potential of the Japanese Economy

THE GROWTH POTENTIAL OF THE JAPANESE ECONOMY

Kenneth K. Kurihara

The Johns Hopkins Press
Baltimore and London

The Johns Hopkins Press, Baltimore, Maryland 21218
The Johns Hopkins Press Ltd., London

Library of Congress Catalog Card Number 75-143329
ISBN 0-8018-1220-8

TO

THE MEMORY OF MY PARENTS

CONTENTS

PREFACE

In the spring of 1965 I had the privilege of serving as a Fulbright Visiting Professor at Tokyo Metropolitan University, which provided the opportunity to visit many other Japanese universities as a guest lecturer. Those professional experiences stimulated me to undertake full-scale research on the growth potential of the Japanese economy, a subject in which I had long been interested and on which I had written from time to time, beginning with the preparation of a paper for the *American Economic Review* in 1946. The present volume might be regarded as the culmination of this endeavor.

The methodological approach here is partly theoretical and partly empirical, in that illustrative formal models are built on empirical foundations while statistical facts are interpreted in a hypothesis-making spirit. To sharpen the issue, international comparisons are made throughout. By way of epilogue an Appendix is provided, consisting of a previously published essay of mine on the possibilities and difficulties of the growing Japanese economy today and tomorrow.

The book offers an analysis of what I consider to be the fundamental forces governing the speed and pattern of Japanese economic growth not only at present but in the decades ahead. I have found myself differing from other writers primarily on the nature of the obstacles to that growth, and here lies the *raison d'être* of a book of this sort. I have freely entered Japan's "growth controversy" here, indicating where and why I dissent from the views of Japanese economists and policymakers. The alternative suggestions and models express my conviction that most of the favorable conditions discussed are indefinitely sustainable, while most of the weak spots are remediable.

The postwar Japanese economy affords a rather unique opportunity to observe and analyze a dualistic pattern of economic development within one geographic entity as well as within one generation. Japan's economic structure still retains some traits of a developing economy while rapidly acquiring the characteristics of a mature "affluent society" and is therefore instructive to both the underdeveloped and the advanced sectors of the world economy. Due emphasis is given to the underlying role of "determinants of determinants" as well as to the functional role of measurable growth variables, for it seemed to me that so idiosyncratic yet so dynamic an institutional-psychological complex as the Japanese economy called for a comprehensive "political economy" approach within a rigorous technical structure. Accordingly, I have endeavored to stimulate broader discussions by appropriate hypothesis-making and parameter-fitting along the way.

A large number of distinguished Western economists have visited postwar Japan and have shown varying degrees of interest in its economic recovery and growth, but they have not commented at any length on its economy. My own research and thinking on the subject has been assisted and clarified by discussions, during and after my Fulbright sojourn in Japan, with Professors T. Shibata and Y. Hayashi of Tokyo Metropolitan University, Professor S. Ichimura of Osaka University, Professor H. Aoyama of Kyoto University, Professor T. Kodera of Kwansei Gakuin University, Professor I. Yamada of Hitotsubashi University, Professor H. Tatusmi of Seikei University, and Professor T. Yamane of Aoyama Gakuin University. I also talked with other economists at these universities; with colleagues at Hiroshima, Sophia, Hokkaido, Otaru Commercial, and Dokkyo universities; and with members of the Japanese Economic Research Center (Nihon Keizai Kenkyu Senta), the Tokyo Finance Association (Kinyu Gakkai), the Japan Management Association (Nippon Noritsu Kyokai), and the Federation of Economic Organizations (Keidanren). To all these and many other Japanese friends I am deeply indebted in countless ways, although they must not, of course, be held responsible for the omissions and commissions of this study, which I hope will repay a small part of the great debt I owe to them. Kiyoshi Abe and Shigeo Minabe, my graduate assistants at the State University of New York at Binghamton, offered knowledgeable comments and helpful suggestions from the Japanese point of view. Finally, I wish to express my gratitude for my late wife's encouragement and support all through the course of this writing.

The Growth Potential of the Japanese Economy

CHAPTER ONE

HIGHLIGHTS OF THE NEW JAPAN'S "MIRACLE GROWTH"

Out of the ruins of a devastating military defeat Japan has dramatically emerged to the incredible position of the fastest-growing nation in the world. This dramatic resurgence of the Japanese economy has been called variously a "miracle," a "secret," and a "paragon." Opinion differs widely, both within and outside Japan, as to exactly what constitutes postwar Japan's "miracle growth" and where it is heading. The answer to the first of these questions entails descriptive generalizations, while the answer to the second involves some new analytical propositions. We shall concentrate on the first of these questions for the moment.

Available data[1] show a panoramic view of postwar Japan's growth performance and potential, summarized in Table 1. A brief interpretation of Table 1 is in order. The 11 percent rate of growth during the 1946-52 period owes its explanation to two extraordinary factors, the extremely low "hand-to-mouth" level of the national income to begin with, and the outbreak of the Korean War in 1950. A vanquished Japan had to start from scratch, albeit with the aid of the benevolent American occupation force. This meant that any absolute increase in the national income (e.g., $\Delta Y = 10$) relative to a low initial level (e.g., $Y = 80$) would give rise to a higher percentage rate of increase (e.g., $\Delta Y/Y = 10/80 = 0.125$ or 12.5 percent) than if the initial

[1] See S. Kuznets, *Six Lectures on Economic Growth* (New York, 1959), and *Postwar Economic Growth, Four Lectures* (Cambridge, Mass., 1965); Japanese Economic Planning Agency, *Keizai Hakusho: Antei Seicho No Kadai* [White Paper on stable growth] (Tokyo, 1965); Federation of Economic Organizations, *Economic Picture of Japan* (Tokyo, 1964), and *Japan Striving for Better Global Co-operation* (Tokyo, 1965); *The Economist* (London), "Year of the Open Door: The Economist Reconsiders Japan," November 28, 1964; Organization for Economic Co-operation and Development, *Economic Surveys: Japan* (Tokyo, 1964 and 1969); United States-Japan Trade Council, *The Dollar and the Yen* (Washington, D.C., 1965); K. Ohkawa, *The Growth Rate of the Japanese Economy since 1878* (Tokyo, 1957); Japan Committee for Economic Development [Keizai Doyukai], "Japan in the World Economy," in Committee for Economic Development, *Japan in the Free World Economy* (New York, 1963); statistical publications of the United Nations and the Bank of Japan; and *Life Magazine*'s special issue on Japan, containing such headings as "Its Astonishing Comeback" and "Its Struggles and Paradoxes," September 11, 1964.

Table 1. Postwar Japan's Growth Record

Selected Period	Real GNP Growth Rate (yearly averages)
	%
1946–52 (recovery period)	11.0 (realized)
1953–58 (normalization period)	7.0 (realized)
1955–62 (liberalization period)	10.3 (realized)
1961–70 ("income-doubling" horizon)	7.2 (expected)

level of income were higher (e.g., $Y = 100$, $\Delta Y = 10$, and so $\Delta Y/Y = 10/100 = 0.1$ or 10 percent). As is well known, the Korean War had a windfall sort of impact on the Japanese economy and, fortuitously, boosted its average annual rate of growth. With the signing of the peace treaty in September 1951, Japan's "recovery period" came to a close, and a new "normalization period" began for the independent Japan.

What is remarkable about this normalization period is that Japan's growth rate of 7 percent, while lower than that of the recovery period, nevertheless was found above the global average, as the United Nations 1958 *Yearbook of National Accounts Statistics* indicates for roughly corresponding years (1951–57): Japan achieved a 7.76 percent rate of growth of real GNP, as compared with West Germany's 7.5 percent, Italy's 5.35 percent, France's 4.64 percent, the United States' 2.93 percent, and Britain's 2.45 percent during the period. The 1955–62 "liberalization period," with all sorts of massive decontrols both at home and abroad, gave renewed impetus to the Japanese economy's "catching-up" process. The new higher average growth rate of 10.3 percent during that period gave birth to the growth controversy mentioned earlier.[2] As for the 1961–70 "income-doubling" horizon, the Japanese Economic Planning Agency cautiously projected 7.2 percent as the probable average growth rate, while Dr. O. Shimomura (the father of the "income-doubling" plan and the initiator of the growth controversy) confidently predicted 10 percent as an achievable average.[3] The realized annual rate of growth for 1963–64 was as high as 14 percent,[4] but whether the ten-year average annual rate envisaged will or will not stay between a maximal figure of 10 percent and a minimal figure of 7.2 percent remains to be seen.

Table 1 can be amplified by the following statistical comparisons of the postwar Japanese economy with other industrial economies: Japan achieved the first place in the international growth race with its 10.3 percent rate of growth of real GNP (1955–62 average), followed by West Germany's 6.7

[2] See M. Shinohara, "The Postwar 'Growth Controversy,' " in his *Growth and Cycles in the Japanese Economy* (Tokyo, 1962).

[3] For some criticisms, see the Appendix to this volume.

[4] See The Japanese Economic Planning Agency's 1965 White Paper.

percent, Italy's 6.2 percent, France's 5 percent, the United States' 3.5 percent, and Britain's 2.3 percent; it took fourth place in industrial production after the U.S., Britain, and West Germany, in that order, in 1963; it placed sixth in foreign trade, following the U.S., West Germany, Britain, France, and Canada, in that order, in 1964; it was first in 1962 gross capital formation, amounting to 35.3 percent of GNP in terms of current dollars, as compared with West Germany's 25.1 percent, Italy's 23.1 percent, Canada's 21.8 percent, France's 17.8 percent, Britain's 16.9 percent, and the U.S.'s 15.8 percent; it took first place in the productivity of capital (marginal ratio of real GNP to fixed capital) in the 1951–57 period, with an estimated figure of 42 percent as compared with West Germany's 36 percent, France's more than 27 percent, Italy's 27 percent, Canada's 19 percent, Britain's more than 17 percent, and the U.S.'s 17 percent; and in 1962 it was second, after the U.S., in the number of patent applications, reflecting its general advance in industrial technology and what are acknowledged to be first-rate techniques with respect to shipbuilding, railway management, manufacture of transistor radios, motorcycles, and cameras (not to mention flower arranging, landscape gardening, technicolor filming, neon advertising, fireworks merrymaking, and other tourist attractions). Impressive as these statistical performances are, they do not penetrate into the recesses of the miracle growth. This is where we must turn to a qualitative interpretation of the quantitative highlights indicated above. I suggest that postwar Japan's economic growth is unique in a number of respects.

1. The Japanese experience demonstrates, for the first time in modern economic history, the feasibility of an economy growing rapidly in spite of scarce natural resources. The permanent loss of colonial sources of raw materials (i.e., Korea, Formosa, Saghalien, and "Manchukuo") intensified the existing scarcity of natural resources in the defeated island nation, and yet Japan surmounted this handicap through the ingenious substitution of technological innovation, manpower utilization, and foreign trade expansion for natural resources. This success defied both the classical dictum that abundant natural resources are a *sine qua non* of economic development[5] and the ideological dogma that a "capitalist" economy can never grow without "colonial exploitation."[6]

2. Japan suffered greater devastation of material and human resources than the other vanquished nations (Germany and Italy). The 1964 Organization for Economic Co-operation and Development report on Japan estimated Japan's wartime loss of capital equipment, not to mention manpower losses, to be 25 percent of the total. These wartime losses did not prevent the

[5] For a neoclassical version see J. Viner, *International Trade and Economic Development* (Oxford, 1952).

[6] For a modern interpretation see P. Sweezy, *The Theory of Capitalist Development* (New York, 1942).

Japanese economy from growing faster than the German and Italian economies, not only by augmenting the quantity of capital but, most important, through a better technical combination of available capital and labor and greater productivities of those factors. These qualitative improvements testify to the Japanese ingenuity and sagacity born of perennial resource scarcity, not to the mere accident of a military defeat. Moreover, the Japanese experience has demonstrated once again the fact that modern wars, short of a nuclear Armageddon, do not destroy those intangible human qualities of the vanquished which ultimately determine the speed and pattern of their economic comeback for better or for worse.

3. The postwar Japanese economy is a conspicuous instance of a mixed public-private economy capable of outstripping centrally planned economies in more ways than one (not just in the speed of growth but also in the consumption of durables like automobiles, television sets, and telephones).[7] Thus the Japanese instance has helped to discredit both the neoclassical orthodoxy that the laissez-faire working of automatic market forces suffices to bring about rapid and stable growth and the Marxian myth that only completely planned economies can raise living standards rapidly. This might come to some readers as a surprise in view of the fact that approximately one-half of Japanese economists are Marxian in orientation, while the rest are neoclassicists and Keynesians. This anomaly seems to owe its being to the delicate and intricate Japanese tradition of state paternalism as a reconciling force, the largely academic nature of Japanese Marxism, without political connections or influences, and the growing appeal of the Keynesian philosophy of a mixed public-private economy to the younger generation of Japanese economists.[8]

4. Japan is the first non-neutral industrial nation to reach in the past hundred years (from 1860 to 1954) the second highest secular growth rate of per capita income, 26.3 percent, as compared with Sweden's 27.6 percent, the U.S.'s 20.3 percent, Russia's 15.4 percent, and Britain's 12.5 percent, according to S. Kuznets' comparative analysis.[9] Had Professor Kuznets' statistical analysis not included the war years, the Japanese figure would have been higher than the 26.3 percent recorded. Contrariwise, Sweden's figure of 27.6 percent (highest in the world) would have been smaller if that country had not been neutral, escaping the unprecedented war damage Japan experienced in consequence of its belligerent status. In view of these qualifications, it is all the more remarkable that Japan recorded the highest secular rate of growth of national income, 42.3 percent, as compared with the U.S.'s 41.2 percent,

---

[7] See "Year of the Open Door," *The Economist*, November 28, 1964.

[8] On such Japanese anomalies see R. P. Dore, "Watakushi No Nihon Keizairon: Nihon Keizaihatten No Shakaiteki Haikei" [My theory of the Japanese economy: The social background of Japanese economic growth], in *Japan Economic Research Center Monthly Report*, September 1965.

[9] Kuznets, *Four Lectures*.

Sweden's 36 percent, Russia's 31 percent, and Britain's 12.5 percent over the same period, according to the Kuznets data (note that Sweden is the only neutral nation among those mentioned here).

5. The postwar Japanese economy has demonstrated the possibility of making greater national welfare compatible with faster economic growth without the traditional *stimulus* of *a military machine*. The Japan of today is the first democratic welfare state to sustain an average annual rate of growth (of real GNP) as high as 9 percent in the twenty years since the end of hostilities in 1945, in contrast to the dependence of prewar Japan's economic development on armament as well as to the apprehensions of militarized nations about the adverse effects of disarmament on their economies. This has refuted in part some observers' prediction that the Japanese economy tended to rely on a warlike atmosphere for its buoyant activity[10] and the suspicion of others that the substitution of welfare for warfare would have the effect of decreasing Japan's private saving and investing propensities via such accompanying welfare measures as greater income-wealth equalization, more social overhead investment, and expanded social insurance programs.

6. The postwar Japanese economy has displayed an endogenous ability to accelerate its growth without secular inflation—to make price stability compatible with rapid growth in a world replete with inflationary tendencies. It has succeeded in maintaining an approximately zero rate of increase in general prices over the past decade (1951–63, to be exact), though it experienced exogenously induced inflations during the 1945–48 period (the result of World War II) and the 1950–53 period (the result of the Korean War). This remarkable stability of general prices in postwar Japan is due largely to the offsetting impact of rising productivity on the movement toward higher wages of organized labor and on the price-administering policy of monopolistic business, especially in those industries which produce most of the items entering the wholesale price index. However, consumer prices have shown an upward trend in recent years, provoking all sorts of "anti-inflation obscurantism" (including bitter charges of a "price-doubling" plot instead of an "income-doubling" plan). Accordingly, the Japanese Economic Planning Agency's 1965 White Paper on stable growth emphasized the urgency of increasing the productivity of the agricultural and tertiary (service) sectors as well as of small-scale manufacturing industries which produce the bulk of goods and services entering the cost of living index. All the same, the amazing fact to be stressed here is that Japan's general price level has remained fairly stable by international standards, to the great benefit of national economic growth and welfare in real terms (i.e., the continuing expansion of real GNP and per capita real income). All this is discussed later in the chapter on inflation (Chapter 9).

[10] See S. Tsuru, "The Strength and Weakness of the Japanese Economy," in his *Essays on Japanese Economy* (Tokyo, 1958).

7. The postwar Japanese economy has proved to be a fruitful testing ground for an experimental pattern of development based on a pragmatic and eclectic blending of diverse ideologies, predilections, and cultures.[11] In contemporary Japan, as in no other nation, Keynes (and post-Keynesians) meets Marx (and Schumpeter), for Japanese social scientists seem to thrive on the combination of a continuing Marxian concern with fundamental institutional reforms and an increasing Keynesian emphasis on technical economic operations.[12] Thus knowledgeable students of the Japanese national character[13] have observed the paradoxical coexistence of such admirable traits as forward-looking *Weltanschauung*, avid curiosity, versatility, diligence, artistic sensitivity, and personal affability on the one hand, and, on the other, such regrettable tendencies as anachronistic insularity, mob fanaticism, civic laxity, traditional cliquishness, consciousness of social class, and undiscerning occidentalism. Nevertheless, the thinking public in postwar Japan seems to be basically united by an overwhelming sense of urgency, a compelling desire for social reform, and a burning ambition to catch up with Western know-how and living standards. Such a basic unity of purpose on the part of the intellectual elite underlies the vitality, adaptability, and potential of the postwar Japanese economy.

[11] The organ of the Center for Japanese Social and Political Studies (in English) and that of the International Institute for Japan Studies (in English) seem to exemplify such an intellectual blending.

[12] See M. Bronfenbrenner, "The State of Japanese Economics," *American Economic Review*, 46 (1956); and S. Tsuru, "Survey of Economic Research in Postwar Japan," *American Economic Review* (Supplement), June 1964.

[13] Compare G. C. Allen, "Factors in Japan's Economic Growth," in C. D. Cowan, ed., *The Economic Development of China and Japan* (London, 1964); Dore, "Watakushi No Nihon Keizairon"; T. Shibata et al., *Sumiyoi Nihon: Kokumin Seikatsu No Shindan* [Toward a livable Japan: A diagnosis of national living] (Tokyo, 1964); S. Ichimura, *Sekai No Nakano Nihon Keizai* [The Japanese economy in the world] (Tokyo, 1965); and the *Life Magazine* special issue, September 11, 1964.

CHAPTER TWO

DEMILITARIZATION AND THE COMPELLING GROWTH DRIVE

It is an irony of history that armament and military successes should have been the principal determinant of prewar Japan's economic development[1] and that a total military defeat in World War II should have spurred postwar Japan's unparalleled economic growth. It is another irony that Commodore Perry should have opened the door of an isolationistic Japan to modern trade and warlike expansion and that General Douglas MacArthur, another American, should have put an end to the ambitions of Japanese militarists and turned the country toward reconstruction and development on the unprecedented constitutional basis of the anti-war clause (Article 9). This chapter will describe the implications of Japan's demilitarization not only for its own economic development but also for the world economy.

Professor S. Tsuru describes prewar Japan's fortuitous dependence on warfare for its economic expansion in these forthright words:

> Japan's economy became thus geared to the high rate of growth which could succeed only on the basis of successive gambles of imperialist character. It will be impossible to narrate the story of Japan's economic development in the modern period without relating it to the successive and successful wars she fought. It meant that the spearhead of her economic development was, on the one hand, the armament and allied industries always generously supported by the state, and on the other, export industries which prospered on the strength of "cheap labor" at home and thanks to the extension of spheres of influence abroad as a result of imperialist conquest. The economy could be highly dynamic so long as Japan fought and won wars.[2]

He skeptically adds:

> New guiding principles for the *defeated* Japan were to be (1) peaceful co-existence with neighboring countries on the basis of equality, and (2) economic democracy as expressed, for example, in the land reform and

---

[1] For prewar growth rates see Ohkawa, *The Growth Rate of the Japanese Economy since 1878.*

[2] Tsuru, *Essays on Japanese Economy*, p. 42.

progressive labor legislations. *And now the mechanism of economic development had to be geared to an entirely new set of precepts: precepts of development in the context of peace rather than in the context of war or of war-like situation.* It was easy enough to say this or write it down on paper; but many of us felt that the required transformation actually involved certain basic changes in Japan's social system.[3]

Professor Tsuru's skepticism about postwar Japan's ability to develop its economic potential without warlike stimulation proved unwarranted. It appears that he overlooked the antinomistic possibility of postwar Japan's economic development being helped rather than hindered by a peaceful environment in general and demilitarization in particular. This point will receive further attention. For the moment, however, the international comparison of defense expenditures given in Table 2 is of interest. The table reveals the striking contrast between Japan's prewar military expenditures and its postwar ones, as well as between the defeated Japan's token defense expenditures and the two victors' substantial military expenditures. The Japanese postwar percentage figure of 1.7 carries with it far-reaching implications for the new Japan's economic growth and welfare. Let me specify and discuss these implications.

Table 2. Defense Expenditures as a Percentage of National Income

Country	Prewar Ratio*	Postwar Ratio**
Japan	7.1%	1.7%
U.K.	3.5%	9.2%
U.S.	1.9%	12.8%

SOURCE: adapted from I. Nakayama, ed., *Nihon Keizai No Seicho* [The growth of the Japanese economy] (Tokyo, 1960), p 16 (the figures cited are based on official statistics of the respective countries).
    *As of 1934–36.
    **As of 1958.

THE END OF TRADITIONAL PYRAMID-BUILDING PUBLIC INVESTMENT

The first and most important single implication of demilitarization is that a far greater proportion of given total capital resources (over and above total consumption) is thereby made available both to purely civilian capital goods industries and to productive social overhead than in the past. Availability of

[3] *Ibid.*, p. 43 (italics mine).

resources for civilian industries is explicitly conducive to private capital formation, while investment in social goals is implicitly beneficial to general productivity. The traditional dissipation of scarce capital resources in the wasteful pyramid-building sort of military investment is permanently over in Japan, thus releasing a quantitatively significant part of investible resources for welfare uses. Military expenditures, while capable of increasing effective demand, nevertheless are incapable of augmenting productive capacity. Moreover, any long-run increase in productive capacity resulting from demilitarization is a permanent net gain to the economy that could never be duplicated by pyramid-building military investment, whereas any short-run reduction of effective demand resulting from demilitarization can be offset by an increase in exports, public welfare expenditures, and private investment.

Unlike newly independent emerging nations, the demilitarized Japan is spared the dubious necessity of choosing between a shiny military jet to impress prestige-conscious neighboring countries and an industrial plant to produce the goods needed at home or abroad. Unlike militarized industrial nations, Japan is also spared the difficulty of producing more and more guns without sacrificing butter. Thus Japan's demilitarization was to be a blessing in disguise, especially from the standpoint of socially optimal resource allocation and capital formation.

THE YOUTHFUL AND PRODUCTIVE CHARACTER OF A LABOR FORCE WITHOUT MILITARY INTERRUPTIONS AND OBLIGATIONS

Not only is the quantity of employable labor increased by permanent demobilization, but the quality of productive labor (between fourteen and fifty-nine years of age in Japan) when fully employed is greatly improved by educational and vocational training uninterrupted by military service, by the full utilization of specialized skills for civilian research and development, and by the selective allocation (based on merit examinations) to growth industries of youthful manpower (especially college graduates) in the absence of compulsory conscription. The vigorous and productive labor force thus made possible is of great practical importance to postwar Japan's growth potential in view of two imminent impediments, an acute shortage of labor in the service and other relatively labor-intensive industries, and a serious productivity lag in agriculture and small-scale industries. These impediments will be amplified in later chapters, but the main point here is that a permanent shift of employable labor from military to civilian employment provides a safety margin against the danger of lagging labor productivity in some sectors of the economy as well as against the danger of full employment labor immobility and scarcity. Needless to say, the new direction of national energies toward creative rather than destructive enterprises is of great intrinsic significance, apart from its implications for the labor force and labor productivity.

THE CIVILIAN INITIATIVE AND FREEDOM FOR
TECHNOLOGICAL PROGRESS

For the first time in modern history, the Japanese "entrepreneur *et hoc genus omne*" finds himself with technological freedom, harnessed in the service of a peaceful economic society. Whereas prewar Japan's technological progress was largely a byproduct of military expansion and arms races, postwar Japan's inventions and innovations are initiated by and for the civilian. While militarized nations the world over waste their technological know-how in the production of weapons of destruction, Japan is in the enviable position of carrying on such fundamental and applied research as is deemed essential to its economic growth and civilian welfare. Thus postwar Japan is generally credited with first-rate industrial know-how, particularly in such peace-oriented areas as shipbuilding, electronics, transistorization, manufacture of photographic equipment and color film, high-speed railways, nuclear research in medicine and industry, high-quality merchandise exports, nationalized tobacco and cigarette production, nationalized central banking, industrial automation and computerization, and application of the tools of mathematical economics and econometrics.

To be sure, postwar Japan is still somewhat behind the technologically highly advanced Western countries, but is catching up in this respect, as well as in other respects, enormously facilitated by the ability to innovate irrespective of military implications or consequences. The initiative for technological progress now lies with the civilian instead of with the military sector, while the nature and direction of that progress are geared to more rapid economic growth and high living standards. The freedom to innovate along non-military lines is an indispensable condition for further economic progress not only in Japan but also in other resource-scarce countries. So crucially important a determinant of economic growth as technological progress cannot and must not be left to the accident and vagaries of warfare, especially in those developing countries which can ill afford the luxury of allocating resources to the production of non-self-liquidating armaments.

THE NEW WELFARE CRITERION OF GOVERNMENT
EXPENDITURE POLICY

Postwar Japan's national budgeting in general and government expenditure policy is rather unique in that it is influenced by the new welfare criterion that few nations can duplicate under prevailing conditions of an uneasy world peace. In the prewar year of 1940, Japan actually alloted as much as 63.8 percent of its national budget (central and local) to military expenditure, while its "defense-related expenditure" in the postwar year of 1960 was 5.9 percent of total government expenditure.[4] Postwar Japan can and does allo-

[4] See K. Takeuchi, "Some Thoughts on the Economic Problems of Contemporary Japan," *Japan Studies*, 1 (1965).

cate the overwhelming bulk of its national revenues from taxes, profits of nationalized industries, and other sources to social security benefit payments, education and culture, research and development, subsidies to private growth industries, and long-range public investment projects of a welfare nature. This means that the tax burden on the populace is no longer so heavy as to impair work incentives and entrepreneurial risk-taking, to the detriment of productivity and growth. This also means that the Japanese taxpayer is now spared the necessity of sacrificing his purchasing power (if not his life as well) for the sake of warfare in general and particularly for the benefit of "dictators and others such, to whom war offers, in expectation at least, a pleasurable excitement."[5]

In this respect, the Federation of Economic Organizations (Keidanren) makes this qualifying observation: "The low rate of defense in the national budget has been distinctive of Japan's national account. However, it may show a considerable rise in the future."[6] The reference to a possible rise in Japan's future defense expenditure relative to the national budget seems to suggest that there will be increasing pressure from some domestic and foreign quarters for a greater self-defense buildup at home and a larger financial contribution to collective-security arrangements abroad. Be that as it may, so long as Japan remains essentially demilitarized, it will gear its expenditure policy (and its tax policy, as a result) to welfare, stability, and growth.

THE FLAG FOLLOWS TRADE, NOT THE OTHER WAY AROUND

Demilitarization of Japan has caused a fundamental change in trade policy from the prewar practice of letting trade follow the flag to the postwar practice of letting the flag follow trade. This new practice is as significant as Britain's postwar decolonization of one area after another to achieve increased and freer trade on an equal basis. When one recalls, with Professor Shinohara, that "the advance of Japan's exports depended to a large extent also on imperialistic aggression"[7] in prewar years, one can readily appreciate the significance of the above change not only for Japan but also for the world economy. Prewar Japan had long been inclined to regard foreign trade as an instrument of military expansionism and had grown accustomed to the acquisition of raw materials by conquest, the acquisition of reparations and indemnities from defeated enemies (e.g., after the Sino-Japanese War and the Russo-Japanese War), and the imposition of Japanese wares on reluctant but weaker trading partners. It took a total defeat in World War II to make Japan realize, for the first time, that a peaceful world is a better place in which to sell and buy, that domestic economic growth is preferable to foreign military aggression for increasing competitive strength in the world market, and that

[5] J. M. Keynes, *General Theory of Employment, Interest, and Money* (New York, n.d.), p. 381.

[6] See Federation of Economic Organizations, *Economic Picture of Japan*, p. 50.

[7] Shinohara, *Growth and Cycles in the Japanese Economy*, p. 66.

the reciprocal expansion of foreign trade in turn promotes domestic economic growth and stability.

As a new member of the International Monetary Fund and the World Bank, Japan stands to enjoy the advantages of autonomous and anonymous multinational borrowing and lending for both short-run external equilibrium and long-run internal development without relying on traditional "beggar-my-neighbor" policies and without the stigma of "imperialism." As a member of the Organization for Economic Co-operation and Development and the Colombo Plan, postwar Japan has an opportunity to help develop nations for a better international division of labor and higher living standards all round. In 1963 Japan's financial aid to developing nations totaled 0.54 percent of the national income.[8] This percentage figure, while short of the 1 percent of national income proposed by the United Nations Conference on Trade and Development (which proposal was supported by Japan as a member nation), nevertheless is a promising start in the direction of greater Japanese participation in the global promotion of trade and development. As a member of the General Agreement on Tariffs and Trade, postwar Japan has an obligation to liberalize its commercial policy (a 93 percent import liberalization ratio had already been achieved in 1965) as well as a right to protest the remaining discriminatory restrictions of other trading nations (especially France, Italy, and England) against its exports.[9] Finally, the demilitarized Japan is freer and more willing to cultivate new markets among the socialist countries without the fear of adverse military and ideological consequences, albeit with some reservations about the quantitative significance of commerce with such state-trading nations.[10]

FURTHER INTERNATIONAL IMPLICATIONS

Japan's mutual security agreement with the United States expires in 1970. Whether Japan will develop its own national defense forces on a full-scale basis or continue to remain demilitarized under American protection beyond 1970 depends on national economic developments as well as the international political climate. In anticipation of the 1970 expiration of the agreement with the U.S., some Japanese strongly favor a constitutional revision to permit Japan's full-fledged rearmament. For instance, former Prime Minister Nobusuke Kishi, in the October 1965 issue of *Foreign Affairs*, argued in favor of such a constitutional revision to "regain [the Japanese nation's] self-confidence and pride." This rearmament sentiment finds its popular expres-

---

[8] See Federation of Economic Organizations, *Japan Striving for Better Global Co-operation*, p. 22.

[9] See CED, *Japan in the Free World Economy*. For Japan's complaints about American protectionism, see United States-Japan Trade Council, *Protectionism in Disguise* (Washington, D.C., 1966), and *The Dollar and the Yen.*

[10] CED, *Japan in the Free World Economy.*

sion in postwar Japan's politico-religious movement called Soka Gakkai (less militant and fanatical than its South Vietnamese Buddhist counterpart). In connection with the growing membership and influence of that nationalistic movement, Professor Y. Seki sounded this warning: "There is always a danger in Japan lest the extremely negative expressions of intellectuals be tied in with the strong, latent feeling of the Japanese people which favors authoritarian leadership."[11] On the other hand, Japan, the only victim of nuclear bombing, is considered so deeply antiwar and antimilitary as to cause Dr. S. Matsumoto (director of the International House of Japan) to observe: "Any person, conservative or otherwise, running for election, has to make speeches supporting this sentiment, if he wants to win."[12]

Some Japanese seem to feel that Japan's pursuit of a completely autonomous and consistent course of diplomatic action is impossible as long as Japan depends on the United States for most of its national defense. Others seem to feel that this lack of autonomy is the necessary price to pay for Japan's continuous economic prosperity, which depends in no small measure upon a profitable American market. It is therefore understandable that any restrictive actions taken by the United States (e.g., a limited list of exports to mainland China, tariff and other barriers against visible and invisible imports from Japan, and the interest equalization tax on Japanese flotations in the American capital market) tend to provoke "anti-American" feelings in Japan.[13] One commentator puts Japan's dilemma thus: "Japan is being forced to seriously consider whether she should sacrifice her autonomy and concentrate upon economic prosperity or strengthen her autonomy at the expense of economic prosperity."[14] The business community and the younger generation in Japan seem to prefer the former alternative, a preference that is in keeping with the increasing willingness of nations to sacrifice a large part of their political sovereignty in the interest of a lasting world peace and an eventual world supergovernment. The partial nuclear test ban treaty among the U.S., the U.S.S.R., and the U.K. concluded in 1963 was a memorable instance of such a willingness on the part of leading world powers. A peaceful and dynamic Japan has much to contribute to global tranquility, stability, and prosperity, especially in this day of increasing international interdependence and complexity.

[11] See his "Japan in Transition," *Journal of Social and Political Ideas in Japan*, August 1964. Also see A. Koestler's description of Soka Gakkai in *Life Magazine's* special issue on Japan (September 11, 1964).

[12] See S. Matsumoto, "Japan and America," *International House of Japan Bulletin*, October 1965.

[13] *Ibid.* See also Federation of Economic Organizations, *Japan Striving for Better Global Co-operation* and United States-Japan Trade Council, *The Dollar and the Yen.*

[14] S. Hayashi, "Autonomous Diplomacy and Defense," *Journal of Social and Political Ideas in Japan*, August 1964.

CHAPTER THREE

THE CHANGING STRUCTURE OF ECONOMIC ENTERPRISE

The speed and pattern of economic growth affect and are affected by quantitatively significant changes in the structure of industry. I shall deal in this chapter with those structural changes in the Japanese economy which seem causally most relevant to its postwar growth potential, to be specific, the changing structure of production, and a shift toward heavy industries and overall growth.

THE CHANGING STRUCTURE OF PRODUCTION

By way of historical perspective, let us begin with an international comparison of major industrial changes in widely separated periods. Table 3 tells an interesting story. Like Britain and America, Japan's historical industrialization is characterized by a structural shift first from land-intensive agriculture to capital-intensive manufacturing and then from the latter to labor-intensive services. The relentless operation of the law of diminishing returns in land-intensive agriculture cannot be completely offset by technological improvements, but the implied domestic shortage of food-stuffs and raw materials can be largely supplemented by expansion of foreign trade under normal conditions. Table 3 shows the predominantly agrarian character of the Japanese economy before the turn of the century, with agriculture constituting as much as 65 percent of national output, whereas Britain's and the U.S.'s agricultural output represented, respectively, 10 percent and 20 percent near the turn of the century.

Turning now to manufacturing, we observe that the contribution of manufacturing industries to Japan's total output nearly tripled in the seventy-seven years from 1878 to 1955, while its American counterpart less than doubled in eighty-five years. Japan's postwar manufacturing contribution to total output lagged behind those of the U.S. and the U.K., as might be expected from its larger agricultural contribution. The Japanese economy, like the British, moved more and more away from land-intensive agriculture toward capital-intensive manufacturing in order to improve its trade position as well as to accelerate its overall industrialization process.

14

Table 3. International Changes in the Structure of Production as a Percentage of Total Output

Country	Period	Agriculture	Manufacturing	Service
Japan	1878-82	65	11	25
	1944-55	24	32	44
U.S.	1869-76	20	21	59
	1947-54	7	38	55
U.K.	1895	10	37	53
	1948-54	6	46	48

SOURCE: adapted from S. Kuznets, *Six Lectures on Economic Growth.*

As for the service column, the following points may be noted. First, Japan's expanding service industries are in line with the general trend toward industrialization, for the greater the degree of industrialization, the greater the need for such services as banking, communications and transportation, insurance, marketing, engineering, advertising, bureaucratic chores, education and welfare, legal counsel, medical care, religious ceremonies, entertainment facilities, hairdressing, and other kinds of more or less labor-intensive activities. Such a need is especially strong if and when an industrialized economy also represents an affluent society with all its cultural and psychological implications. With the exception of relatively capital-intensive communications and transportation, the services enumerated above are by nature labor-intensive and hence do not lend themselves readily to factor substitution (e.g., by capital), though automation and computerization might be operative in some limited cases. This creates some formidable difficulties on the supply side of a growing economy, as will be discussed in a later chapter. Second, the postwar contribution of service industries to total output in the U.S. and the U.K. is greater than that in Japan, even if it is secularly somewhat less in those countries than before the turn of the century. Thus Britain's postwar figure is 48 percent and that of the U.S. 55 percent, whereas Japan's figure is 44 percent. Third, the fact that around one-half of total output is contributed by service industries in Britain and America might well be one explanation for the relatively slow growth of the British and U.S. economies in the postwar period, inasmuch as the productivity of service industries as a whole is generally lower than that of manufacturing industries everywhere. This implies that if and when Japan's service industries catch up with their British and American counterparts in scope and extent, its postwar growth will, ceteris paribus, decelerate. I shall return to this last point later.

Professor K. Ohkawa's statistical study, which shows the following structural changes in the postwar Japanese economy considered by itself, is summarized in Table 4. It tells us substantially the same story as does Table 3.

Table 4. Structural Changes in the Postwar Japanese Economy

Industry	Period	Output Ratio
		%
Agriculture	1946	38.8
	1955	21.9
Manufacturing	1946	26.3
	1955	30.1
Service	1946	34.9
	1955	48.0

SOURCE: adapted from Ohkawa, *The Growth Rate of the Japanese Economy since 1878.*

Here again we see the ascendance of manufacturing and service industries at the expense of agriculture during the postwar period 1946–55. Japanese manufacturing industries as a whole accounted for almost one-third of the total, as compared with a little over one-quarter in 1946; service industries increased their contribution to 48 percent, which figure is comparable to those of the U.S. and the U.K. in Table 3; the declining trend in the agricultural contribution is expected to continue, to the dismay of the rural population and the alarm of urban planners.

What worries Japanese economists and policymakers is not the decline of agriculture per se (which they take as an inevitable concomitant of industrialization) but the implied emergence of new impediments to sustained prosperity and growth for the economy as a whole. Such impediments take many forms, e.g., a reduction of domestic self-sufficiency in foodstuffs (especially rice production) that may or may not be offset by expansion of foreign trade; a vote-oriented farm support policy coupled with irrational protectionism in behalf of high-priced domestic farm products, all tending to increase consumer prices; depletion of agricultural labor reserves that might not be easily compensated for by increased productivity; a mass exodus of youth from rural areas that tends to reduce agricultural productivity and to intensify the already serious problems of Japanese urban centers.[1] Some of these points will be discussed subsequently and in later chapters.

To make matters worse, the postwar preponderance of service industries evidenced in Table 4 carries with it some ominous implications for Japan's growth potential. While this is a common feature of all advanced industrial societies, the Japanese case is exceptionally detrimental to sustained growth for a number of idiosyncratic reasons. First, the preponderance of service

[1]See T. Shibata, *Sekai No Toshio Megutte* [World metropolises] (Tokyo, 1964); S. Ichimura, *Sekai No Nakano Nihon Keizai*, esp. chap. 5.

industries prematurely and precariously changes Japan's production function from a capital-dependent one to a labor-dependent one, that is, from $Y = K/b$ to $Y = N/v$ (where Y is total output, K is capital input, N is labor input, b is the capital-output ratio, and v is the labor-output ratio), since the quantitatively significant substitution of capital for labor is made so difficult by largely labor-intensive service industries as to render labor the scarcer factor, or $N/v < K/b$. This shift is premature because the Japanese economy still has plenty of scope for roundabout methods of production; it is precarious because a chronic shortage of labor (instead of capital) may well become the principal bottleneck on the supply side of sustained growth.

A second cause for alarm over the growth of service industries is that it tends to push arbitrary distribution to the point where the incomes earned in those industries may have little relation to productivity, thus jeopardizing the whole system of functional distribution as well as making for structural cost-push inflation. Third, they aggravate the traditional redundancy of tradesmen and middlemen, the allocation of resources to overduplicating, overspecializing services, and the misdirection of productive energies to unskilled or semi-skilled "white-collar" labor markets (as witnessed, for example, by the crowd of clerks in business offices, the overflowing bureaucrats in government offices, and the hordes of hostesses in countless bars).

A SHIFT TOWARD HEAVY INDUSTRIES AND OVERALL GROWTH

The most striking instance of the dynamic interaction of industrialization and rapid growth can be seen in postwar Japan's structural shift toward heavy industries which constitute the kernel of modern economic expansion. The structural shift in industrial production is reflected in a similar change in the composition of Japanese exports, as shown in Table 5. Since heavy industries

Table 5. *Structural Shifts from Light to Heavy Industries in Postwar Japan*

Product*	Percentage of Total Output		Percentage of Total Exports	
	1950	1959	1950	1960
Light	50.0	36.5	67.2	51.8
Heavy	50.0	63.5	32.8	48.2

SOURCE: adapted from CED, *Japan in the Free World Economy.*
*Light industrial products include textiles, foods, and ceramics, while heavy industrial products include chemicals, machinery, and metals.

are capital-intensive, an increase in their output implies more capital goods for producers, more machine-made goods for consumers, better technological know-how all around, and more complementary trade with non-industrial trading nations. Let us pursue these implications a bit further.

The capital-intensive character of heavy industries (larger K relative to any given N in K/N, where K and N are, respectively, capital input and labor input) is evidenced not only by the roundabout methods of production involved but also by the rising trend of investment in those industries. The percentage of total investment going to heavy industries in 1962 reached 63.8,[2] a figure which could easily be inferred from the 63.5 figure in 1959 shown in the table. The greater availability to the consumer of machine-made products because of this increase is shown in the rise of the durable consumer goods production index from 33 in 1950 to 557 in 1962 (calculated with 1955 as the base year).[3] Postwar Japanese consumers have become as "gadget-happy" as those in other advanced industrial societies, for better or for worse. Machine-made consumer durables, while not always superior to hand-made ones in quality, nevertheless make a quantitatively significant contribution to consumer welfare in general. We shall elaborate on this point in a later chapter on the changing pattern of consumption. Further evidence of the technological progress implied in Table 5 is the increased use of foreign techniques (i.e., patented inventions) from 174 applications for machine industries and 176 for chemical industries in the 1950–57 period to 592 for the former and 356 for the latter in the 1958–63 period.[4] It is therefore plausible to infer that heavy industries played a leading role in the rise of overall manufacturing productivity from an index number of 74 in 1951 to 159 in 1961 (base year is 1955).[5]

While Japan's exports of light industrial products still have a slight edge over heavy industrial products (see Table 5), the latter increased from 32.8 percent in 1950 to 48.2 percent in 1960. This shift in the nature of Japanese commodity exports is causing a corresponding shift in their direction: over two-thirds of Japan's machinery and apparatus exports in 1963 went to nonindustrial nations,[6] whereas the bulk of its prewar exports to such nations consisted of light industrial products.[7] The increasing shift of Japanese exports toward heavy industrial products is all the more important not only because those products are complementary to non-industrial nations' exports of primary commodities, and Japanese industrial products are becoming increasingly competitive, but also because the trend in postwar Japan powerfully contributes to export-biased technological progress as well as to import-substituting industrialization, thereby strengthening its competitive position

---

[2] Federation of Economic Organizations, *Economic Picture of Japan*, p. 5, based on the Japan Development Bank investment survey.

[3] CED, *Japan in the Free World Economy*, p. 56.

[4] Ichimura, *Sekai No Nakano Nihon Keizai*, p. 145, based on a Finance Ministry foreign investment survey.

[5] CED, *Japan in the Free World Economy*, p. 45.

[6] Federation of Economic Organizations, *Economic Picture of Japan*.

[7] For prewar export data, see Shinohara, *Growth and Cycles in the Japanese Economy* (esp. chap. 3).

in the world market. It is not surprising, therefore, that Japanese exports during the ten-year period 1953 to 1963 expanded at the average annual rate of 14.7 percent, by far the highest expansion among the industrial trading nations.[8]

Table 6 gives additional insight into postwar Japan's industrial potential. It tells something about what Japanese economists call *Nijyu kozo* ("dual structure"), defined by Professor M. Shinohara as "an economy in which modern (or capitalistic) large firms co-exist with pre-modern (or pre-capitalistic) medium and small firms, and in which there prevail enormous wage or income differentials not found in more advanced countries."[9] The coexistence mentioned by Professor Shinohara is rooted in the peculiarly Japanese *oyabun-kobun* ("master-protégé") relationship handed down from feudal days. Thus small firms serve large ones as subcontractors, parts producers, or even subsidiaries, remaining an integral part of "the vertical hierarchy of big and medium-sized firms" in a rather subtle fashion. Whereas big business in other industrial countries tends to drive small firms out of existence (in the absence of some public intervention) or, at best, to merge them into bigger combines (within the limits of anti-trust laws), its Japanese counterpart in the postwar (as well as prewar) period takes a "live and let live" paternalistic attitude toward small firms, albeit for pragmatic reasons. These reasons are summarized by Professor Shinohara thus: "The existence of the dual economy makes it possible for the relatively large firms to employ cheap labor in combination with highly advanced technological production methods. The combination of cheap labor and high-level technology tends to reduce costs and raise profits, thus leading to greater capital financing from internal funds, on the one hand, and a lowering of product prices on the other, which in turn helps to expand the foreign markets."[10]

I do not myself believe that the Japanese economy can count on the existence of the "dual structure" for future national comparative advantages in the world market or stable growth at home. Already horizontal integration

Table 6. *Employment and Productivity Differentials between Large- and Small-Scale Industries*

Scale of Enterprise	Proportion of Industrial Employment		Average Annual Productivity	
	1948	1959	1948	1959
Large	43.8%	44.3%	1.00%	2.46%
Small	56.2%	55.7%	1.00%	1.00%

[8] OECD, *Economic Surveys: Japan* (1964).
[9] See his *Growth and Cycles in the Japanese Economy*, p. 14.
[10] *Ibid.*, p. 21.

is spreading in the form of supermarkets and department stores, and its vertical integration at the manufacturing level is likely to proceed along Western lines of oligopoly and oligopsony. This implies that the Japanese economy, no less than other advanced market economies, will depend more and more on a delicate balance of power among big business, organized labor, and the national government for its smooth functioning.

Table 6 also shows that more than half of total industrial employment goes to small enterprises with less than a hundred employees. This fact has at least two implications: there is considerable "disguised unemployment" that might be shifted to more productive large-scale industries without thereby reducing the total output of small-scale industries, and small-scale industries can and must adopt more capital-intensive production techniques in order to take advantage of economies of scale. The table further indicates great disparities in productivity between large and small industries and between 1948 and 1959. Whereas small industries' productivity remained constant between the two periods, large industries' productivity more than doubled, suggesting that they are more than twice as productive as small ones and that their productivity is capable of increasing even more rapidly as time goes on. This last observation throws light on Japan's international position as depicted in Table 7.

Table 7, in conjunction with Table 6, reveals a causally significant correlation between the rate of growth of industrial productivity ($\Delta\rho^m/\rho^m$) and the rate of growth of real GNP ($\Delta Y/Y$) in Japan, in relation to other industrial nations. It suggests that the Japanese economy was able to achieve the highest rate of growth of real GNP during the 1951–57 period mainly because of its high rate of growth of industrial productivity recorded for the 1950–60 period. Any significant discrepancy between these two rates ($\Delta\rho^m/\rho^m$, $\Delta Y/Y$), as in the cases of Japan and Canada, can be explained by the offsetting influence of the rates of growth of agricultural and service productivities ($\Delta\rho^a/\rho^a$, $\Delta\rho^s/\rho^s$ not shown in Table 7) or by the rate of growth of the work force ($\Delta N/N$, which is a co-determinant of $\Delta Y/Y$). In the Japanese case, we may hypothesize that a high rate of growth of productivity in manufacturing industries (such as the 12.2 percent figure in Table 7) is offset by low rates of growth of agricultural and service productivities, reducing the overall rate of growth of productivity ($\Delta\rho/\rho$) and hence the rate of growth of real GNP to 7.76 percent in Table 7, although it is higher than those of other industrial nations, given the rate of growth of labor population ($\Delta N/N$).

We have discussed the structural changes in the Japanese economy mainly from the supply side, but there remain some significant structural changes on the demand side. The next two chapters will deal with those changes.

Table 7. International Rates of Growth of Industrial Productivity and GNP

Country	Industrial Productivity Growth Rate (1950–60 average)*	Real Gross National Product Growth Rate (1951–57 average)**
	%	%
Japan	12.2	7.76
Italy	7.6	5.35
France	5.8	4.64
West Germany	5.1	7.50
Netherlands	4.9	5.25
Sweden	3.0	3.80
U.S.	2.7	2.93
Canada	2.5	4.21
U.K.	2.3	2.45

SOURCE: UN, *Yearbook of National Accounts Statistics*, and OECD, *General Statistical Bulletin*.

*Denoting industrial (manufacturing) output by Y^m, labor input used in manufacturing industries by N^m the average productivity of labor in those industries by ρ^m, and the rate of growth of industrial productivity by g^m, we may show the relations involved in the first column as follows:

$$\rho^m = \frac{Y^m}{N^m}, \ \rho_t{}^m = \rho_0{}^m (1 + g^m)^t, \ g^m = \frac{m_t}{m_0} - 1. \quad (t = 0, 1)$$

**Considering the GNP supplied as the equivalent of total productive capacity (as distinguished from effective demand), the rate of growth of productive capacity ($\Delta/Y/Y$) in any capital-abundant, labor-scarce industrialized economy (where capital cannot be bodily substituted for labor for structural reasons) equals the sum of the rate of growth of labor productivity and the rate of growth of labor population:

$$\frac{\Delta GNP}{GNP} \equiv \frac{\Delta Y}{Y} = \frac{\Delta \rho}{\rho} + \frac{\Delta N}{N}, \quad (\rho \equiv Y/N)$$

where $\Delta\rho/\rho$ is the overall rate of growth of labor productivity, $\Delta N/N$ is the overall rate of growth of labor population (productive), and ρ is the overall productivity of labor (of which ρ^m is the most important component).

CHAPTER FOUR

SHIFTING PATTERNS OF CONSUMPTION AND SAVING

"Consumption," said Keynes, "is the sole end and object of all economic activity."[1] How does postwar Japan's economic growth fare in this respect? How has the pattern of consumption demand changed in postwar Japan? What are the implications of structural changes in consumption demand for Japan's growth potential in the future? We seek answers to these questions in the first part of this chapter. Has Japan's traditional thriftiness been drastically modified by postwar conditions? What are some of the more important institutional-psychological factors affecting postwar Japan's savings habits? Will postwar Japan remain a "high-saving" nation? How would a changing pattern of saving affect Japan's future economic growth? The second part of this chapter will attempt to provide answers to this set of questions.

THE SHIFTING PATTERN OF CONSUMPTION

The Japanese economy's pattern and standard of consumption are in a rapid process of transition, revealing both strengths and weaknesses from the standpoint of stable growth and mass welfare. Japanese economists seem satisfied with the observed fact that postwar Japan's rapid economic growth has been achieved without imposing belt-tightening on the consuming public or lowering per capita consumption,[2] while foreign observers seem impressed by the postwar Japanese consumer's increasing appetite for Veblenian "conspicuous consumption," apparently without changing his instinctive savings habits.[3] It looks as though postwar Japan combines the best of two worlds, the world of consumer sovereignty and the world of consumer welfare. Actually, such will not be found to be the case, for a number of reasons specified in this section.

[1] Keynes, *General Theory of Employment, Interest, and Money*, p. 104.
[2] The most optimistic and complacent view will be found in O. Shimomura, "Hatashite Bokoki Ka?" [Is the Japanese economy in the "historical ascendency" period?], in Nakayama, ed., *Nihon Keisai No Seicho*.
[3] *The Economist* (London), "Year of the Open Door."

22

Since per capita consumption is the best single index of general consumer welfare, let us look at postwar Japan's consumption trend. Table 8 indicates that consumption per capita in postwar Japan is strongly correlated with its GNP per capita decade after decade, the former increasing *pari passu* with the latter. However, the table conceals both the autonomous (non-income) factors affecting the rising trend of consumption per capita and the welfare content of the consumer goods involved. Moreover, the much higher per capita consumption projected for 1970 relative to per capita GNP implies a secular fall in the rate of population growth and of personal saving that may well affect Japan's future growth adversely. We would need more data than provided by Table 8 in order to see these concealed elements, even though we may appreciate the doubling of per capita consumption during the 1950–61 period as a remarkable step forward in general consumer welfare.

Table 8. Per Capita Income and Consumption Trends

Period	Per Capita Consumption*	Per Capita Nominal GNP*
1950	71 (realized)	70 (realized)
1961	142 (realized)	171 (realized)
1970	263 (projected)	272 (projected)

SOURCE: the figures for 1950 and 1961 are based on data from the Bank of Japan, the Bureau of Statistics, and the office of the Prime Minister; the 1970 figures are those projected in the Economic Planning Agency's 1970 *New Long-Range Economic Plan of Japan*.
    *Base year, 1955.

There are at least three ways to treat consumption expenditure in greater detail in order to see more clearly the influences of autonomous factors, the standard of consumption, and the welfare content of consumer goods and services. Leaving the first of these for the later discussion of the consumption ratio, the other two can be discussed here. The Engel coefficient in Table 9 refers to the ratio of food outlays to total private consumption expenditure. As might be expected of a more and more affluent consuming public anywhere, the Engel coefficients in Table 9 indicate the Japanese consumer's increasing ability to shift secularly from the "health and decency" standard to the "comfort" standard. To reach the "luxury" standard attributed to the U.S., the U.K., Canada, Switzerland, and Sweden, Japan's real GNP would have to grow much faster than in the past and reduce the Engel coefficient more drastically than shown in Table 9.

More interesting is the "new living mode" index in Table 9, a weighted index which represents and measures qualitative changes in the consumption pattern of postwar Japan. The qualitative changes so measured are, to cite a few conspicuous examples, from rice to bread, from *sashimi* (raw fish) to

Table 9.   *Shifts in the Consumption Pattern*

Economic Indicator	Statistical Index* 1953	1961
Engel coefficient	45	38
New living mode	65	1,168

SOURCE: Japanese Economic Planning Agency's 1962 White Paper on national living.
*Base year, 1955.

hamburgers, from *sake* to whiskey, from consumer non-durables to consumer durables, from homemade clothing to readymade clothing, from *kimono* to Western clothes, from a middle-school education to a college education, from trains to jet planes, from streetcars to taxicabs, from public buses to private automobiles, from surface mail correspondence to air mail, from jazz to classical music, from doubling up with parents to independent apartment living, from toil to recreation, etc. The inordinate upward shift of this latter index from 65 in 1953 to 1,168 in 1961 eloquently attests to the postwar Japanese consumer's radically changed habits and tastes as well as his greatly improved welfare in terms of the more and better goods consumed and the finer things of life enjoyed.

Despite the greater consumer well-being evidenced in the table by the Engel coefficient and the index of new living mode, the postwar Japanese consumption standard is still behind those of more affluent Western nations. Western visitors to Japanese homes cannot help but notice how sparse is the use of modern equipment and gadgets, such as family cars, refrigerators, air conditioners, central heating systems, flush-toilet systems, telephones, and washing machines, in comparison with their own countries.[4] It is therefore refreshing that Professor T. Shibata and his colleagues should have written a self-critical symposium entitled *Sumiyoi Nihon* (Toward a Livable Japan) with the subtitle *Kokumin Seikatsu No Shindan* (A Diagnosis of National Living). Understandably, some Japanese economists defend the inadequacy of Japanese household equipment and the paucity of modern devices as an inevitable concomitant of an investment-geared growing economy, but I myself am inclined to criticize it as a sad commentary on the welfare content of the fast growing GNP and to pinpoint it as a *reason* for even more rapid overall growth. I believe, with Keynes, not only that consumption is the ultimate object of production but also that economic progress is helped rather than hindered by more and better consumption in the long run.[5]

[4] For international comparisons of rates of ownership of consumer gadgets, see *ibid.*, p. 1007. The countries involved are Japan, the U.S., the U.K., Germany, France, and the U.S.S.R. during the 1957–63 period.

[5] See his "The Propensity to Consume," in *General Theory of Employment, Interest, and Money*, esp. p. 106; also "Economic Possibilities for Our Grandchildren," in *Essays in Persuasion* (London, 1952).

More important from the standpoint of stable growth is the expansion of the consumer demand for durables in postwar Japan. Both the output and ownership indices of consumer durables in Table 10 imply quantitatively significant changes in the structure of consumption demand in postwar Japan,

Table 10. Production and Ownership of Consumer Durables

Period	Output Index of Consumer Durables*	Ownership of Representative Consumer Durables as Percentage of Urban Family Owners**				
		Refrig- erators	Washing Machines	Vacuum Cleaners	TV Sets	Sewing Machines
1950	33					
1960		15.7	45.4	11.0	54.5	71.7
1961	705					
1963		51.9	70.2	37.4	91.3	81.3

*See Table 8 for sources of data. Base year, 1955.
**Adapted from Federation of Economic Organizations, *Economic Picture of Japan.*

so much so that the cyclical instability and cycle sensitivity of the Japanese economy are greater than before World War II.[6] The durability structure of consumption demand is now added to that of investment demand (especially for plant and equipment) to intensify the periodicity and amplitude of the trade cycle, thus aggravating the problem of "cyclical growth" common to all advanced market economies. The 1964 OECD report on the Japanese economy went so far as to suggest that Japan's principal cycle-maker in the future might well be consumption demand rather than investment demand. Interestingly enough, the 1965 Economic Planning Agency White Paper on national living expressed the view that each saturation round of demand for consumer durables is accompanied by a structural imbalance between effective demand and productive capacity, to the detriment of stable growth.[7] If the Japanese economy succeeds in sustaining stable growth (with a minimum of periodic recessions and inflations) despite the destabilizing influence of the income-price elastic demand for consumer durables, then investment demand (private and public) and exports may have to be viewed as exercising a counterbalancing influence on the growth of effective demand relative to that of productive capacity. Thus the increasing ownership of refrigerators. washing

[6] See H. Aoyama, ed., *Nihon Keizai To Keiki Hendo* [The Japanese economy and the trade cycle] (Tokyo, 1957); Shinohara, *Growth and Cycles in the Japanese Economy.*

[7] The imbalance in question might be expressed in the inequalities

$$\left(\frac{dY^d}{dt} = \frac{1}{s}\frac{dC}{dt}\right) \lessgtr \left(\frac{dY^s}{dt} = \frac{1}{b}\frac{dK}{dt}\right),$$

where Y^d is effective demand, Y^s is productive capacity, C is autonomous consumption, K is real capital, s the savings ratio, b is the capital-output ratio, and t is time.

machines, and other consumer durables shown in Table 10, while conducive to greater consumer well-being, nevertheless aggravates the antinomic problem of maintaining stable growth in postwar Japan.

Finally, let us ponder the future pattern of consumption in the Japanese economy, shown in Table 11. The consumption-income ratio (average propensity to consume) is important for the light it throws on the proportion of total resources available to the capital goods industries in a given period, as well as on the contributing share of consumption demand to aggregate effective demand in the same period. I interpret the secular fall in consumption-income ratio shown in the table as reflecting both the gradual satisfaction of the extraordinary postwar pent-up demand in about 1950 and the lingering impact of the 1954 and 1957–58 recessions before 1960, the preparatory year of the so-called income-doubling plan. The 59 percent figure projected by the Economic Planning Agency for 1970 seems to be a plausible extrapolation of the past consumption trend, but it seems to underestimate the trend value of the consumption ratio by overlooking some far-reaching autonomous shift parameters affecting the consumption function. Powerful forces of an institutional-psychological nature are operative in postwar Japan such that the consumption function is likely to shift upward secularly, contrary to the impression given by Table 11. Subject to econometric testing,[8] I suggest that the following forces will tend to increase Japan's future consumption ratio,

Table 11.   The Consumption Ratio

Period	C/GNP*
1950	62.3% (realized)
1960	54.6% (realized)
1970	59.0% (projected)

SOURCE: the figures for 1950 and 1960 are based on data from the Bank of Japan, the Bureau of Statistics, and the Office of the Prime Minister; the figure for 1970 is based on the 1961 projection of the Economic Planning Agency.

*Consumption expenditure (C) here refers solely to private outlays for consumer goods and services, excluding government consumption.

that is, beyond the target year of 1970 used in the Economic Planning Agency's projection:

(1) the income-equalization trend incident upon welfare statecraft, rising trade unionism, and greater productivity of medium- and small-scale indus-

[8] What must be tested is $\partial C/\partial \gamma_i (i = 1, \ldots, n)$ where γ's are the shift parameters in question. In this connection, Professor Shinohara, for example, tested various income hypotheses (e.g., absolute and relative) relative to the consumption ratio but not such hypotheses as I offer above concerning the possible effects of shift parameters. See Shinohara, *Growth and Cycles in the Japanese Economy* (esp. chaps. 9 and 10).

tries, tending to redistribute income from profitmakers to wage-earners with a higher marginal propensity to consume, and thus making for larger total consumption expenditure relative to any given GNP;

(2) the enlargement of consumer credit incident upon "credit living" that depends more and more on installment and credit-card buying, automobile loans, home improvement loans, etc., tending to increase the positive intercept (with zero income) and so to shift the entire consumption function upward;

(3) greater reliance on progressive income taxes (at present nearly 60 percent of total public revenue) coupled with less reliance on regressive sales and other indirect taxes (at present some 40 percent of total revenue), tending to encourage consumption demand as well as to enhance the welfare and equity of consumers as taxpayers.

(4) technological progress in the direction of supplying more and cheaper consumer durables (especially such newcomers as family cars[9] and electric washing machines), tending to intensify the consuming public's quest for gadgetry and modernity.

(5) the expansion of mass advertising via such mass communication media as television commercials, radios, the press, window displays, and billboards, tending to inspire the competitive spirit of status symbolism in the consuming public;

(6) the rising trend of urbanization because of industrial concentration in metropolitan areas (especially Tokyo, Osaka, Nagoya, Kobe, and Sapporo), tending to foster pretentious and conspicuous consumption and hence to increase the already high marginal average propensity to consume among urban consuming units;[10]

(7) the institutionalization of interdependent consumption based on the psychology of keeping up with domestic and foreign Joneses, and facilitated by mass communications and transportation media, tending to strengthen the so-called "demonstration effect" on a technologically and sociologically ever shrinking world of consumers.

If my prediction of a higher consumption ratio for Japan proves wrong, I must plead in advance that some unforeseen trend may have come into play or that something may have gone astray with econometric testing of the hypotheses. I might add the observation that Keynesian and Marxian economists in Japan see eye to eye on the theoretical possibility of "underconsumption" militating against prosperity and equity. [11]

---

[9] Japan is the fourth largest automobile producer in the world, but poor roads and highways as well as high prices of cars seem to limit domestic sales at present. See United States-Japan Trade Council, *United States Trade with Japan: 1960–64* (Washington, D.C., 1966).

[10] See Shinohara, *Growth and Cycles in the Japanese Economy*, p. 48.

[11] See S. Tsuru, *Essays on Marxian Economics* (Tokyo, 1956). In this connection, the reader of Keynes's *General Theory* will recall this sympathetic word on underconsumptionists: "It may be convenient at this point to say a word about the important schools of thought which maintain . . . that the chronic tendency of contemporary societies to underemployment is to be traced

THE SHIFTING PATTERN OF SAVING

Analysis of the behavior of saving is important for the light it throws on the leakage involved in the short-run multiplier expansion of effective demand[12] as well as on the leverage involved in the long-run growth of productive capacity.[13] As is well known, Keynes concentrated on the former, while Harrod emphasized the latter. In the present context, I am more concerned with the post-Keynesian treatment of saving as a resource-releasing force than with the Keynesian treatment of it as a demand-decreasing force. To be more specific, I am interested in those aspects of postwar Japan's institutional-psychological complex which fundamentally change its national habit of thrift and hence affect the Japanese economy's potential ability to expand its capital stock.[14]

Let us begin with a preliminary quantitative discussion by reference to Table 12. It shows Japan to be the highest among the "high-saving" nations in the postwar period and reveals a number of interesting facts about Japan's savings pattern relative to those of other nations. First, Japan's total national savings relative to GNP depends far more heavily on personal than on corporate or budgetary savings, reflecting the operation of the classical "abstinence of the rich" principle of accumulation based on great income disparities. Second, the relatively small contribution of corporate savings to Japan's national savings in terms of ratios reflects the traditional reliance of Japanese firms on external financing (especially long-term bank loans) for business expansion (especially new fixed investment in plant and equipment). Third, the relatively heavy contribution of budgetary surpluses to Japan's national savings in terms of ratios reflects the paternalistic role of the state as a saver

---

to underconsumption. . . . In existing conditions . . . where the volume of investment is unplanned and uncontrolled . . . these schools of thought are, as guides to practical policy, undoubtedly in the right" (pp. 324–25).

[12] That is, s is involved in the multiplier equation $\Delta Y = 1/s(\Delta I)$, where Y is effective demand, I is autonomous investment, s is the marginal propensity to save, and $1/s$ is the multiplier (= k). As such, s is a leakage coefficient that limits the expansionary power of investment demand (ΔI).

[13] That is, s is involved in the growth of productive capacity given by $g = s/b$ where g is the rate of growth of productive capacity (and real capital) or $\Delta Y/Y$ (= $\Delta K/K$), s is the average propensity to save ($S/Y = \Delta S/\Delta Y$ when a long-run linear saving function with a zero intercept is assumed), and b is the average marginal capital-output ratio ($K/Y = \Delta K/\Delta Y \equiv I/\Delta Y$). As such, s is a leverage coefficient in the sense that the growth rate (g) is an increasing function of s though a decreasing function of b ($\partial g/\partial s > 0, \partial g/\partial b < 0$).

[14] Professor Shinohara mentions some interesting idiosyncratic factors affecting postwar (as well as prewar) Japan's saving; see his *Growth and Cycles in the Japanese Economy*, pp. 280–83. My own list of relevant factors will be somewhat different from his, especially because I am concerned with a longer future horizon than he is. What Shinohara limits to personal savings habits, namely, a tendency among Japanese people to regard consumption, not saving, as "the residual" ($C = Y - S$ instead of $S = Y - C$), might well be extended to Japan's corporate and budgetary savings policies, at least in spirit (even though investment would have to be substituted for consumption in the case of corporations). This point is discussed in detail above.

Table 12.   International Postwar Savings Ratios

Country	Savings as Percentage of Real GNP*			
	Personal	Corporate	Budgetary	Total
Japan	10.0	3.9	6.7	20.6
U.S.	5.2	2.3	2.3	9.8
U.K.	2.7	4.8	—	7.5
France	3.1	2.4	2.2	7.7
West Germany	9.4		8.0	17.4

SOURCE: adapted from I. Nakayama, *Nihon Keizai No Seicho*, p. 26.

*The original figures are related to Gross National Expenditure (GNE), but inasmuch as GNE = GNP *ex post* I have related them to GNP here. The figures are the 1951–57 averages and are based on Japanese Planning Agency and United Nations data.

in general and its small government expenditures on military and welfare items relative to tax and other public revenues. Last, Japan's high savings ratio reflects its corresponding high rate of growth of real income, since the higher the rate of growth (g) the higher the savings ratio (s) will have to be, given the capital-output ratio (b), according to $g = s/b$ and $s = bg$, or $S/Y = (I/\Delta Y)(\Delta Y/Y)$.

Two rather exceptional patterns of saving for the U.K. and West Germany are represented in Table 12: the former's corporate savings ratio exceeds its personal saving ratio, and the latter's budgetary savings ratio constitutes nearly one-half of its aggregate savings ratio. Perhaps Britain's low personal savings ratio reflects its extensive welfare state measures that tend to obviate the usual saving for "a rainy day," while its high corporate savings ratio may be due to a general policy of relying on internal more than on external financing for business expansion. The figure for the American corporate savings ratio would normally be higher than shown in Table 12 inasmuch as persistent budgetary surpluses as a source of national saving are the exception rather than the rule in the United States. The relatively low personal savings ratio of 5.2 for the U.S. may be a reflection of the fact that existing income disparities are moderate because of strong sentiment in favor of ever greater "equality of opportunity."

Let us now discuss the "high-saving" Japanese economy from the standpoint of personal thriftiness. Table 13 suggests that the relatively high personal savings ratio in 1950 reflected not only the traditional thriftiness of the Japanese as a nation but also the uncertainties surrounding the period from 1946 to 1952. Those uncertainties were partly real and partly anticipatory, for the 1951 peace treaty and the end of the American occupation were expected to generate apprehensions about a new independent Japan. The traditional thriftiness involved here derives from the dual influence of the Buddhist teaching of frugality as a transcendental virtue (analogous to the

Table 13. *Personal Saving in Postwar Japan as Percent of Disposable Income*

Period	Savings Ratio*
1950	14.7 (realized)
1960	20.0 (realized)
1970	15.0 (projected)

SOURCE: adapted from CED, *Japan in the Free World Economy*. See Table 11 for statistical sources.

*The personal savings ratio is usually defined as $S^p/(Y - T + R)$, where S^p is personal savings out of disposable income $(Y - T + R)$, Y is national income, T is income taxes, and R is government transfer payments.

Puritan influence that prevailed in Western countries) and the calamity-ridden nature of the island nation (earthquakes, typhoons, floods, etc.), necessitating saving for "rainy days" as a matter of course.

The higher figure of 20 percent in 1960 might well be partly the result of the greater sense of insecurity which the recessions of 1954 and 1957–58 had generated and perpetuated and partly, perhaps, of the emergence of "stock-mindedness" among Japanese savers around 1955, who began to save in the new form of securities rather than in the old form of bank deposits.[15] However, the high savings ratio recorded for 1960 was not regarded as a trend, for the Economic Planning Agency's projected figure for 1970 represents a considerable drop from the 1960 figure. Yet the projected 1970 figure may turn out to be an upward-biased extrapolation of the past trend, for it is likely that beyond 1970, if not by 1970, Japan's institutional-psychological complex will have undergone such changes as to decrease rather than increase the personal savings ratio, albeit perhaps not to so low a level as in Western industrial societies.

This brings me to some hypotheses for the consideration of Japanese econometricians and policymakers with respect to those forces in postwar Japan which are likely to reduce its propensity to save in the future, in addition to those affecting the propensity to consume discussed above.

1. Perhaps the most compelling reason for a declining savings ratio (regarded as the sum of the personal, corporate, and budgetary savings ratios) in the future Japanese economy (beyond the "income-doubling" terminal year 1970) is, in my view, twofold, namely, a lower rate of growth of real income and a higher productivity of capital, which between them make for a lower savings ratio as a long-run desideratum or *sine qua non*. Suppose that the

[15] *Ibid.*, p. 282.

future rate of growth of output desired or projected averages 5 percent per annum and that the future productivity of capital desired or projected averages 50 percent. Then the required savings ratio will be 10 percent, according to the familiar Harrod-Domar growth formula $\Delta Y/Y = (S/Y)/(I/\Delta Y)$ where $\Delta Y/Y (\equiv g)$ is the average annual rate of growth of national output, $S/Y (\equiv s)$ is the average savings ratio, and $I/\Delta Y (\equiv \Delta K/\Delta Y = K/Y \equiv b)$ is the marginal average capital-output ratio. That formula gives us the transpose

$$s = \frac{S}{Y} = \frac{\Delta Y/Y}{\Delta Y/I} \equiv \frac{g}{\sigma} = \frac{0.05}{0.50} = 0.1,$$

where σ is the reciprocal of the capital-output ratio, or $\sigma = 1/b = 1/2 = 0.5$. The above formula is based on the assumption that the savings ratio is an increasing function of the rate of growth of real income but a decreasing function of capital productivity, or $\partial s/\partial g > 0$, but $\partial s/\partial \sigma < 0$. It indicates the theoretical possibility of the future Japanese savings ratio declining secularly as a consequence of a lower rate of growth of output (either desired as a matter of policy or occasioned by endogenous developments) and a higher productivity of capital (desired or occasioned in a similar way). This implies both that the future investment ratio (I/Y) would be lower than at present and that the future consumption ratio (C/Y) would be higher[16] as a matter of social priority:

$$\frac{I}{Y} = \frac{I}{\Delta Y}\frac{\Delta Y}{Y} = 2 \times 0.05 = 0.1 \text{ and } \frac{C}{Y} = 1 - \frac{I}{Y} = 1 - 0.1 = 0.9.$$

2. One of the most powerful forces making for a smaller personal savings ratio in postwar Japan is the gradual extension of the social security program with respect to both coverage and benefit payments. In keeping with the universal drive toward welfare statism[17] postwar Japan is slowly but surely moving in the direction of a more comprehensive and adequate system of social insurance that tends to obviate traditional thriftiness to a considerable degree. Rather less compelling saving for amenities (e.g., for home ownership, the education of children, and the purchase of new cars) will sooner or later

[16] The actual consumption ratio (C/Y) would be smaller than the 90 percent figure indicated in this illustration because the government-expenditure ratio $(\overline{G}/Y)$ and the export ratio $(\overline{X}/Y)$ would have to be subtracted from 1:

$$\frac{C}{Y} = 1 - \frac{I}{Y} - \frac{\overline{G}}{Y} - \frac{\overline{X}}{Y},$$

which is based on $Y = C + I + \overline{G} + \overline{X}$ of the mixed open economy.

[17] For international comparisons of the ratio of the cost of social security to national income, see International Labour Organization, *The Cost of Social Security* (Geneva, 1958).

supersede the rather more compelling saving for security (e.g., against un-employment, sickness, and indigence in old age) in Japan, as is already taking place in advanced Western societies with extensive social security programs. The relative underdevelopment of social insurance in Japan has hitherto been tolerated on the dubious ground that strong family ties presumably provide an automatic guarantee of private economic security, but the feudalistic family system is breaking down rapidly in postwar Japan. Some welcome the change as presaging the Western type of individualism, in the best sense of that term (the intrinsic dignity and liberty of the individual), while others resist it as ushering in the perverse type of individualism devoid of the tradi-tional respect for parental authority, the clannish protection of "poor rela-tions," and the sacrificial spirit of altruism toward other members of one's family and community.[18] The development of social insurance will un-doubtedly accelerate the breakdown of the traditional family system, for better or for worse. The main point here is simply that the comprehensive program of social insurance under way in postwar Japan, however motivated or actuated, will have the long-run effect of diminishing Japan's personal savings ratio insofar as it is related to the traditional habit of saving for a rainy day.

3. Another force making for a smaller savings ratio in postwar Japan is the quantitatively significant redistribution of income from high- to low-income brackets which its new democratic egalitarianism and more homogeneous industrial structure are bound to bring about on an increasing scale. In Japan, as in other countries, low-income groups as a whole have a lower marginal propensity to save than high-income groups as a whole, judging from an official survey of patterns of saving by occupation.[19] Accordingly, any per-sisting redistribution of income from high-income groups with a high marginal propensity to save would entail a low savings ratio for the whole economy.[20]

---

[18] See Dore, "Watakushi No Nihon Keisairon"; T. Shibata et al., *Sumiyoi Nihon*; Ichimura, *Sekai No Nakano Nihon Keizai*; K. Tange, "Urbanization and Japanese Culture," *International House of Japan Bulletin*, August 1965.

[19] Statistics Bureau, Prime Minister's Office, *Chochiku Doko Chosa* [A survey of savings behavior] (Tokyo, 1959). The data are in terms of average savings ratios, but we may assume long-run savings functions with a zero intercept for all occupational groups involved so as to make the average and the marginal savings ratio equal.

[20] The mechanism involved can be illustrated thus:

(1) $Y = W + Q$,

(2) $W/Y = \delta$, $Q/Y = 1 - \delta$,

(3) $S = S_w + S_q$,

(4) $S_w = s_w W = s_w \delta Y, (s_w \equiv \Delta S_w / \Delta W)$

(5) $S_q = s_q Q = s_q (1 - \delta) Y, (s_q \equiv \Delta S_q / \Delta Q)$

(6) $s_w < s_q$,

(7) $S = s_w \delta Y + s_q (1 - \delta) Y = [s_w \delta + s_q (1 - \delta)] Y$,

This is so whether such an income redistribution is the result of more progressive income taxes, more welfare subsidies (transfer payments) to low-income families, the greater bargaining power of a fully employed labor force, the greater productivity of wage-earners in small-scale industries, the more aggressive high-wage movement of organized labor, more stringent anti-monopoly laws, or a combination of all these factors.

4. The last trend to be mentioned here is an increasing institutional-psychological tendency for a growing middle class to hold liquid or near-liquid assets, such as savings accounts, bonds, and insurance policies.[21] The larger the total volume of such institutional nesteggs in the hands of consumers, the greater the psychological impact of price changes or changing nominal asset holdings on the personal savings ratio for the whole economy. The so-called Pigou effect may come of age in the future Japanese economy so as to reduce the savings ratio, albeit not in the way originally envisaged by A. C. Pigou. According to Pigou, savings is a decreasing function of real consumer assets as well as an increasing function of income:

$$\frac{\partial S}{\partial \left(\frac{A}{p}\right)} < 0, \quad \frac{\partial S}{\partial Y} > 0.$$

Here S is personal savings, A is consumer assets in money terms, and p is the general price index. The "Pigou effect" expressed by the first of the above functions is based on the familiar law of diminishing marginal utility, namely, the greater are the initial holdings of consumer assets in real terms, the smaller the additional utility or satisfaction derived from additional saving in the form of such assets (saving for amenity) will be. Applied to the future Japanese economy, this may mean that savings will decrease $[\Delta S(t) < 0]$ if the volume of consumer assets increases $[\Delta A(t) > 0]$ with constant prices $[\Delta p(t) = 0]$ or if general prices decrease $[\Delta p(t) < 0]$ with constant asset holdings $[\Delta A(t) = 0]$. Since general prices are unlikely to decrease secularly in the future Japanese economy, it may be more plausible to assume that a

---

(8) $S/Y = s_w \delta + s_q(1 - \delta)$.

Here Y is real national income, W wage-income, Q profit-income, S total saving, S_w saving out of wage-income, S_q saving out of profit-income, δ the wage-income distribution ratio (representing low-income brackets), $1 - \delta$ the profit-income distribution ratio (representing high-income brackets), s_w the marginal propensity to save out of wage-income, and s_q the marginal propensity to save out of profit-income. Given the basic assumption expressed by (6), a *higher* wage distribution ratio $[\Delta \delta(t) > 0]$, however brought about, would *decrease* the overall saving ratio given by (8), that is, $\Delta s(t) < 0$, where $s \equiv S/Y$.

[21] See Shinohara, *Growth and Cycles in the Japanese Economy*, pp. 237–50.

downward Pigouvian effect on saving will arise mainly from an increase in the volume of nominal asset holdings. Even if secular inflation were to occur, asset holdings in the special form of stocks as an inflation hedge (A') might increase so as to decrease saving relative to any level of national income. This functional interdependence between A' and p ($\partial A'/\partial p > 0$ when A' is specified as consisting of inflation-hedging stocks) was not considered by Pigou, but it might apply to the Japanese case in the future.

CHAPTER FIVE

PRIVATE INVESTMENT AND
SOCIAL OVERHEAD CAPITAL

The Japanese Economic Planning Agency's 1965 White Paper was, for the first time, explicitly concerned with stable growth, abandoning its previous concern with accelerated growth pure and simple. This suggests a growing awareness of the "dual character" of investment among Japanese economists and policymakers. Up to the present Japan has represented a capital-scarce, labor-abundant economy and therefore has understandably been preoccupied with the capacity-creating aspect of investment. However, the Japanese economy will increasingly find itself concerned with the more difficult task of bringing the demand-generating aspect of investment into equilibrium with its capacity-creating aspect—of balancing the demand and supply sides of capital accumulation in order to achieve stable growth without serious inflationary and deflationary periods.[1]

[1] The following demonstration may be useful:

(1) $Y^s = f(N, K)$

(2) $Y^s = \frac{\partial Y^s}{\partial N} N + \frac{\partial Y^s}{\partial K} K$

(3) $\frac{dY^s}{Y^s} = \frac{\partial Y^s}{\partial N} \frac{N}{Y^s} \frac{dN}{N} + \frac{\partial Y^s}{\partial K} \frac{K}{Y^s} \frac{dK}{K}$

(4) $dY^s/Y^s \equiv g^s$, $dN/N \equiv n$, $dK/K \equiv k$, $(\partial Y^s/\partial N)(N/Y^s) = \mu$, $(\partial Y^s/\partial K)(K/Y^s) = \eta$

(5) $g^s = n + k$ (rate of growth of productive capacity)

(6) $Y^d = c(1 - z - m)Y^d + \bar{I} + \bar{G} + \bar{X}$ $(\bar{I} \equiv dK)$

(7) $dY^d = c(1 - z - m)dY^d + \overline{dI} + \overline{dG} + \overline{dX}$

(8) $dY^d/Y^d \equiv g^d$, $\overline{dI}/Y^d \equiv \pi$, $\overline{dG}, \overline{dX} = 0$

(9) $g^s = \pi[1 - c(1 - z - m)]^{-1}$ (rate of growth of effective demand)

(10) $g^d - g^s = 0$; $\pi[1 - c(1 - z - m)]^{-1} = \mu n + \eta k$ (dynamic equilibrium condition)

implying $g^d - g^s > 0$ (inflationary divergence) and $g^d - g^s < 0$ (stagnationary divergence). Here Y^s is productive capacity, Y^d is effective demand, N is labor input, K is capital input, g^s is the rate of growth of productive capacity, g^d is the rate of growth of effective demand, n is the rate of growth of labor input, k is the rate of growth of capital input, μ is the productivity

In this chapter the behavior and structure of investment in the growing Japanese economy will be analyzed with an eye to the future. Because of the increasing emphasis given to growth and welfare in present-day Japan as well as in other affluent societies, the analysis will be carried on under the two headings of private investment and social overhead capital.

PRIVATE INVESTMENT

Let us begin our discussion by examining Table 14. The table provides some insight into the structure and behavior of Japanese investment. It shows the overwhelming predominance of private over public investment during the period surveyed, much to the delight of those relying on private enterprise for rapid growth and to the dismay of those depending on public policy for that purpose. This preponderance of private investment was maintained at the expense of residential and public investment, just when postwar Japan's needs for individual housing and social overhead capital were becoming so acute as to evoke this poignant remark from Professor Ichimura: "Our country has sacrificed housing and postponed social overheads in favor of private investment in equipment, which has played a starring role in its rapid growth; this [social] irrationality cannot go on!"[2] The private investment in equipment

---

elasticity of labor input, η is the productivity elasticity of capital input, c is the marginal propensity to consume domestic goods out of disposable income, z is the marginal income tax rate, m is the marginal propensity to import, π is the ratio of additional investment to effective demand; $\bar{I}$, $\bar{G}$, and $\bar{X}$ are autonomous net investment, autonomous government expenditure, and autonomous exports, respectively.

Here equation (1) expresses a linear homogeneous production function based on the simplifying assumptions of constant returns to scale and the unitary elasticity of factor substitution. Equation (2) re-expresses (1) via Euler's theorem. From (2) and its differential we can derive equation (3), which is simplified as equation (5) by reference to the denotations given by (4). Equation (5) represents the supply side of a growing economy, and it shows the operational importance of the *rate of growth of capital input* (dk/K) among the independent variables. Additional capital input (dK) represents the capacity-increasing aspect of net investment (I) which appears on the demand side of the economy via equation (6) and its indicator $(I = dK)$. Equation (6) expresses the familiar Keynesian income-expenditure relation in the broad context of a mixed open economy. From the differential of (6) given by (7) and the definitions and assumptions specified by (8), we derive the rate of growth of effective demand expressed by (9). Equation (9) represents the demand side of the growing economy, and it shows the operational significance of the ratio of additional net investment to effective demand $(d\bar{I}/Y^d = \pi)$ as a determinant. Additional net investment $(d\bar{I})$ represents the demand-expanding multiplicand *à la* Keynes. Equation (10) expresses the dynamic equilibrium condition to be satisfied for stable growth, and it implies the possibilities of an inflationary divergence due to $g^d > g^s$ and a stagnationary divergence due to $g^d < g^s$.

[2] This is a translation of Professor Ichimura's comment in his *Sekai No Nakano Nihon Keizai*, p. 160. He implicitly questions the wisdom of Japan's continuing to maintain a high rate of economic growth at the cost of social welfare in general, for housing and social overhead capital certainly have a vital bearing on general welfare. In this connection, the reader might be interested in my "Social Overhead Capital and Balanced Economic Growth," *Social and Economic Studies*, September 1970.

Table 14. Components of the Investment Ratio

| Year | Private Investment | | | Public | National |
	Residential	Equipment	Total	Investment	Total
	%	%	%	%	%
1960	2.3	20.8	23.1	9.1	32.2
1961	2.4	23.1	25.5	9.7	35.2
1962	2.8	19.2	21.0	11.5	33.5
1963	3.1	18.2	21.3	11.6	32.9
1970					31.0

SOURCE: the figures for the 1960-63 period represent the ratios of investments to Gross National Expenditure and are adapted from Ichimura, *Sekai No Nakano Keizai*, p. 160. The non-disaggregated figure for 1970 represents the ratio of investment to Gross National Product projected in the Japanese Economic Planning Agency's 1961 *New Long-Range Economic Plan of Japan*.

column shows remarkable stability in terms of ratios, implying a persistent business buoyancy irrespective of cyclical setbacks.[3] This stability has misled Dr. O. Shimomura, the theoretical father of Japan's income-doubling plan (1961-70), to overestimate the productivity coefficient for the planning horizon by including only that investment in his calculation,[4] however. The Planning Agency's projected figure of 31 percent for 1970 (which is the terminal year of the income-doubling plan), while still high by international standards, nevertheless seems to be an overoptimistic extrapolation from the past trend which ignores structural assumptions about the prospective nature of the investment function. Such a high investment ratio for 1970 and thereafter does not seem to me to be consistent with the policy shift from rapid growth to stable growth emphasized in the 1965 White Paper of the Planning Agency or with the changing pattern of consumption discussed in the previous chapter.

Last, a persistently high national investment ratio (as shown in the last column of the table), whether primarily the result of private or public investment, is both the cause and the effect of Japan's high rate of economic growth, ceteris paribus. It can be shown that this is not at all circular reason-

[3]Mr. Hisao Kanamori, chief of the research section of the Japanese Economic Planning Agency, called attention to the anomalous phenomenon of investment in private equipment increasing by as much as 21 percent (of GNP in money terms) even during the recession period 1964-65. (See his contribution to the symposium on the 1965 White Paper in *Japan Economic Research Center Monthly Report*, September 1965.)

[4]Dr. Shimomura arrives at his productivity coefficient thus: $\Delta GNP = \sigma I_F(1 - r)$; $\Delta GNP/GNP = \sigma(1 - r)(I_F/GNP)$; $\sigma = (\Delta GNP/GNP)[1/(1 - r)]$ (GNP/I_F), where GNP is Gross National Product, I_F is private equipment investment, r is the ratio of replacement investment to total private equipment investment, and σ is the productivity coefficient in question (capital productivity in his special sense). I shall criticize all this in a later chapter on technology. (See Shimomura's remarks in Nakayama, ed., *Nihon Keizai No Seicho*, pp. 159-60.)

ing. First, assume the basic investment function of the simple form $I = b\Delta Y$, where I is national investment (private and public), Y is GNP, and b is the capital coefficient (marginal = average). Dividing that investment equation by Y, we get $I/Y = b(\Delta Y/Y)$, showing the possibility that the higher the investment ratio (I/Y), the higher the rate of growth of GNP $(\Delta Y/Y)$, given a constant capital-output ratio $[\Delta b(t) = 0]$. Considered as the dependent variable (the unknown), the investment ratio is thus mainly the effect of the rate of growth of GNP (an independent variable, in this case). If the capital coefficient (b) should decrease for some reason, the investment ratio would also decrease to that extent even if the rate of growth of GNP remained persistently high. Turning now to the investment ratio regarded as a causal factor,[5] this time we may assume the investment ratio and the capital coefficient as given (i.e., as the known independent variables to determine the unknown—the rate of growth of GNP, in this case). Then we get $\Delta Y/Y = 1/b(I/Y)$, where $1/b$ is the productivity of capital. This transposed growth equation shows the theoretical possibility of GNP growing more rapidly as a consequence of a higher investment ratio $[\Delta(I/Y)_t > 0]$, given the constant productivity of capital $[\Delta(1/b)_t = 0]$. Further, assuming with Harrod and Domar that the saving-investment equilibrium condition is satisfied in an *ex ante* sense, $S/Y = I/Y$, then we get the familiar Harrod-Domar growth equation $\Delta Y/Y = s/b = \sigma s$, where $s = S/Y$ and $\sigma = 1/b$.

It is interesting, in this connection, to make an international comparison of investment ratios and growth rates. Let us pursue the analysis further. Table 15 reveals a number of pertinent facts which require analysis. First, and most obvious, Japan and West Germany, which were growing faster than the other industrial nations selected, also represented economies with extraordinarily high levels of investment. Since the capital coefficients for Japan and Germany during the 1951–57 period averaged 2.53 and 2.77, respectively,[6] we may infer that the higher GNP growth rate for Japan was largely the result of its higher investment ratio and, in part its higher productivity of capital (or, what amounts to the same thing, its lower capital-output ratio), according to the aforementioned formula $\Delta Y/Y = 1/b(I/Y)$. Second, and less obvious, the relatively low GNP growth rates for the U.S. and the U.K. must not be simply explained in terms of their relatively low investment ratios, for those low GNP growth rates were also caused by their low productivities of

---

[5] Failure to clarify the precise cause-and-effect relationship between investment and growth results in a rather platitudinous or rhetorical extollation of investment as the key to "accelerated economic growth" or an implicit faith in the spurious statistical correlation between investment and growth. Such a failure is exemplified by Governor N. A. Rockefeller's otherwise fine *Accelerated Economic Growth* (Cooperstown, N.Y., 1960), which generously praises Japan's high investment and growth.

[6] Calculations of the capital coefficients are provided by Professor M. Shinohara and are based on UN data; see Nakayama, ed., *Nihon Keizai No Seicho*, p. 13.

Table 15. International Investment Ratios and GNP Growth Rates (1951–57 averages)

Country	Fixed Investment Ratio	Inventory Investment Ratio	Total Investment Ratio	GNP Growth Rate
	%	%	%	%
Japan	21.6	6.8	28.4	7.76
U.S.	16.7	1.3	18.0	2.93
U.K.	14.4	1.5	15.9	2.45
France	17.2	1.0	18.2	4.64
West Germany	20.8	2.5	23.3	7.50

SOURCE: data are from the UN's 1958 *Yearbook of National Accounts Statistics* and the Japanese Economic Planning Agency's White Papers. The figures for investment ratios relate respective investments to real GNP, while those for growth rates represent the average annual rates of increase in real GNP.

capital (the capital-output ratios for the U.S. and the U.K. during the same period averaged 5.67 and 5.61, respectively[7]). This implies the long-run importance of modernizing and streamlining plant and equipment so as to increase the productivity of capital (in other words, to decrease the capital coefficient) not only in such "catching-up" countries of Japan and Germany but also in such mature industrial nations as Britain and America.[8] I shall return to this matter in a later chapter on technology.

Third, Table 15 shows that Japan's inventory investment ratio is far higher than those of the other industrial countries covered. Professor M. Shinohara has explained this peculiarity of Japanese investment largely as a reflection of Japan's high growth rate, which tends to increase business confidence in the safety and profitability of holding large inventories.[9] Be that as it may, what Professor Shinohara has not explained is the dangerous long-run implication of a high inventory investment ratio for the stable growth of the Japanese economy, even though he recognizes the seriousness of "inventory cycles" in Japan.[10] A high inventory investment ratio tends to affect both the supply and the demand side of a growing economy in a destabilizing way. It affects the supply side adversely by reducing fixed investment relative to any given output and hence the overall productivity of capital, which depends primarily on durable plant and equipment—so much so that Professor E. Domar has

---

[7] *Ibid.*

[8] Governor Rockefeller, in his advocacy of "accelerated economic growth" as "a key to the American future," complains that "our replacement investment has not been sufficient over many years to keep our overall stock of production facilities from perceptibly aging year by year" (*Accelerated Economic Growth*, p. 17). For a British counterpart, see T. Barna, *Investment and Growth Policies in British Industrial Firms* (London, 1962).

[9] Shinohara, *Growth and Cycles in the Japanese Economy*, p. 155.

[10] *Ibid.*, pp. 163ff.

deliberately limited his famous "sigma effect" (capital productivity) to fixed capital.[11] If Japan has thus far maintained a high productivity of capital despite its high inventory investment ratio, it is because of such offsetting practices as the "rationalization" of replacement investment and the productivity-oriented (in distinction to cost-oriented) formation of capital in general. A high inventory investment ratio also affects the demand side of a growing economy adversely by increasing that part of total investment relative to any given effective demand which is particularly cycle-sensitive.[12] In the case of the Japanese economy, this may mean that small firms, to whose great number Professor Shinohara partly attributes Japan's high inventory investment ratio[13] and which are exceptionally vulnerable to cyclical bankruptcy,[14] are allowed to exercise an unduly destabilizing influence on the growth of effective demand, keeping it in equilibrium with that of productive capacity via the stability condition $i/s' = s/b$ (see footnote 1 above). However, there are hopeful indications that greater business integration (vertical and horizontal), less dependence on imported raw materials, better transportation facilities, better marketing and distributing techniques, and other structural changes will make for a smaller and smaller inventory investment ratio in Japan[15] until it is reduced to the level prevailing in more advanced industrial countries.

Last, Table 15 conceals the percentage contributions of public investment to fixed investment (see the first column without a private vs. public breakdown), especially in the cases of Japan and the U.K. Because of exceptionally large nationalized industries (e.g., railways, television broadcasting, and central banking) in those countries, it would be misleading to infer from the table that private investment was solely responsible for their fixed investment ratios, to the exclusion of the unspecified contribution of public fixed investment. One source credits Japan's public fixed investment with more than 10 percent of its GNP in 1965 and Britain's with about 7.5 percent[16] (figures higher than those for the U.S., France, or West Germany).

What of Japan's future investment ratio in general and its future private investment ratio in particular? The answer to this question must go beyond

[11] Domar, "Expansion and Employment," *American Economic Review*, March 1947, p. 68.

[12] The Japanese Economic Planning Agency's research head, Mr. Kanamori, for instance, acknowledged the causal significance of inventory investment for the 1964–65 recession. See his symposium contribution in Nayakama, ed., *Nihon Keizai No Seicho.*

[13] *Ibid.*, p. 155.

[14] The bankruptcy cases of medium- and small-sized firms were running at the rate of five hundred per month during the 1964–65 recession. See Kanamori's article in *ibid.*

[15] See M. Kojima, "Jyuyo Kozo No Henka Ni Tekio Shita Hanbai Kihan O" [Toward a marketing structure appropriate to the changing structure of demand], in *Japan Economic Research Center Monthly Report*, September 1965.

[16] See Federation of Economic Organizations, *Japan Striving for Better Global Co-operation*, p. 17.

any simple extrapolation from the past; it requires a number of structural-behavioral assumptions about the prospective determinants of investment regarded both as a source of effective demand and as a creator of productive capacity. I find myself rather skeptical about the possibility of achieving and maintaining such a high overall investment ratio as the Japanese Economic Planning Agency estimated for the terminal year of the income-doubling plan, that is, 31 percent for 1970. Even if Japan's investment ratio were to turn out to be as high in 1970 as the Planning Agency optimistically envisages, it would probably decline thereafter, for reasons to be specified subsequently. I am even more skeptical about the prospect of Japan's private equipment investment ratio remaining as high as in the past, that is, around 20 percent (see Table 14). Let me spell out the reasons for my skepticism.

1. The overall investment ratio required to sustain Japan's rate of growth of output (real GNP or NNP) is likely to decline considerably below the 31 percent figure projected by the Planning Agency, especially beyond 1970, if for no other reason than that the rate of growth of output regarded as a policy desideratum or a probable datum is itself likely to decline.[17] Given the basic investment function of the form $I = b\Delta Y$, we have seen that the investment ratio is capable of decreasing as a consequence of a fall in the rate of growth of output when the capital-output ratio remains constant:

$$\left(\frac{I}{Y}\right)^r_t = b\left(\frac{\Delta Y}{Y}\right)^t; \quad \Delta\left(\frac{I}{Y}\right)^r_t < 0 \text{ if } \Delta g_t < 0 \text{ and } \Delta b_t = 0.$$

Here $(I/Y)^r$ is the required investment ratio, $(\Delta Y/Y)$ is the rate of growth of output, b is the capital-output ratio, and $g = \Delta Y/Y$, while the subscript t is time. Suppose, for example, that Japan's average annual rate of growth of output (GNP) beyond 1970 turns out to be 5 percent, instead of the 7.1 percent figure estimated by the Planning Agency for the 1960–70 period, and that its capital-output ratio remains constantly at 2.5 (which is slightly lower than the figure of 2.53 estimated by Professor M. Shinohara for the 1951–57 period[18]). Then the above formula will give us a figure of 12.5 percent as the required investment ratio, a figure which is drastically smaller than the 31 percent figure envisaged by the Planning Agency for 1970.

2. Contrary to the above constancy assumption about the secular behavior of the capital-output ratio, Japan's future capital coefficient is likely to fall for a number of specific reasons.[19] First, Japan's continuously high rate of

---

[17] For detailed explanations of the declining value of Japan's growth rate see the next chapter and the Appendix.

[18] The Shinohara calculations appear in Nakayama, ed., *Nihon Keizai No Seicho*, p. 13.

[19] This matter will be taken up in greater detail in a later chapter on technology and productivity.

growth of output itself tends to make for the presence of excess capacity as a normal phenomenon via the mechanism of $s/b - i/s' > 0$ (or simply $\Delta Y^s/Y^s > \Delta Y^d/Y^d$) discussed in footnote 1 above. The presence of excess capacity in turn tends to reduce the inducement to invest via the nonlinear investment function of the form $I = f(Y, K)$ based on the assumptions $\partial I/\partial Y > 0$ and $\partial I/\partial K < 0$.[20] Second, as noted earlier, Japan's industrial structure is rapidly changing in the direction of less capital-intensive industries, i.e., tertiary or service industries requiring more labor than capital per unit of output. Even the exceptionally capital-intensive transportation and communications facilities included in the generally labor-intensive tertiary sector of the economy are likely to require less capital per unit of output if the present technological trends of transisterization and computerization persist in the future. Third, the productivity of capital is likely to increase so as to reduce the amount of capital required per unit of output, not only because of a more efficiency-conscious replacement investment policy but also because of technological and other improvements in the quality of capital input. For these and other specific reasons (some of these other reasons are mentioned in the next section of this chapter), Japan's future capital-output ratio is likely to decline rather than to rise. If so, the aforementioned formula will give us a smaller required investment ratio than the Japanese Economic Planning Agency would have us believe, for that formula tells us:

$$\Delta\left(\frac{I}{Y}\right)^r_t < 0 \text{ if } \Delta b_t < 0 \text{ while } \Delta g_t = 0.$$

3. The ratio of private equipment investment to GNP, which has thus far remained fairly stable at about 20 percent (see Table 14), is also likely to decline beyond 1970. We can already detect from Table 14 a trend toward a larger private residential investment ratio as well as a larger public investment ratio (including social overheads). Allusion has been made to postwar Japan's crying need for more houses and more social overhead capital. Should the Japan of tomorrow decide to allocate more of its given capital resources to individual housing and social overhead capital formation as a matter of public policy, the private equipment investment ratio would have to decline in favor of a higher private residential investment ratio and a higher public investment ratio. We derive from the identity $I \equiv I_f + I_h + I_g$ (where I is national total investment, I_f is private equipment investment, and I_g is government investment) the following relation in terms of ratios:

$$\frac{I_f}{Y} \equiv \frac{I}{Y} - \frac{I_h}{Y} - \frac{I_g}{Y},$$

[20] See my "An Endogenous Model of Cyclical Growth," *Oxford Economic Papers*, October 1960.

which indicates the possibility that, ceteris paribus, the private equipment investment ratio may decrease $[\Delta(I_f/Y)_t < 0]$ as a consequence of hypothetical increases in the private residential investment ratio and the public investment ratio $[\Delta(I_h/Y)_t, \Delta(I_g/Y)_t > 0]$. Such a theoretical possibility will have to be taken into account if a more realistic estimate of Japan's future capital coefficient or capital productivity is to be made, for these changes in the components of the total investment ratio, while they do not affect that ratio itself, nevertheless can significantly influence the trend value of capital productivity and hence its reciprocal, the capital coefficient.

4. Assuming that inventory investment will become as negligible in the future Japanese economy (for the reasons already indicated) as in the Western industrial countries, we may plausibly equate Japan's total private investment with its private fixed investment (in durable plant and equipment). Then Japan's total private investment ratio is likely to become smaller after 1970 than the average figure of 22.7 percent for the 1960–63 period (calculable from data in Table 14) would indicate. Such a likelihood can be envisaged thus: let us assume, with Keynes, that private investment (I) is an increasing function of the marginal efficiency of capital (e) and a decreasing function of the rate of interest (r), that is, $I = f(e, r)$, where $\partial I/\partial e > 0$ and $\partial I/\partial r < 0$. The marginal efficiency of capital in postwar Japan has hitherto been so much higher than the rate of interest that its capital goods industries have tended to expand their investment activity largely through high interest-bearing bank credits.[21] This has been so much the practice that Japan's business economists (and academic economists, to a lesser degree) are beginning to express their great apprehensions about the adverse impact of what they call *shihonkosei akka* (a worsening of the financial-capital structure) on future private investment activity as well as on Japan's future stable growth.[22] The marginal efficiency of capital is bound to decline inversely with the rising stock of durable capital assets, especially in the capital-abundant decades ahead, yet the rate of interest is unlikely to fall significantly, in large part because of Japanese policymakers' perennial concern with balance of payments deficits in general and specifically with the danger of short-term capital moving abroad to money centers paying higher interest. In such circumstances the private inducement to invest would be reduced relative to GNP, to the detriment of Japan's future stable growth—unless its public investment ratio could be expected to rise in a manner which would offset it exactly.

5. According to Table 12 in the preceding chapter, Japan's total private savings ratio (personal and corporate) was 13.9 percent on the average for the

[21] See Y. Yamamoto, of the Japanese Economic Planning Agency, "Business Profits and Capital Structure," in *Japan Economic Center Monthly Report*, September 1965.

[22] See a joint article by Y. Uchiki of the Fuji Bank, A. Kanai of the Mitsubishi Bank, and S. Kawai of the Tokyo Electric Co., in *ibid.*, p. 89ff.

1951–57 period covered, while Table 15 above gives the average figure of 28.4 percent as its.private investment ratio for the same period. This implies that the Japanese economy has thus far been able to maintain a high private investment ratio well in excess of its prevailing private savings ratio, contrary to the condition of savings-investment equilibrium in the conventional sense ($S - I = 0$, in terms of ex ante private saving and investment activities). Let me be a bit more specific. Suppose that the "savings-investment" equilibrium condition to be satisfied by the Japanese economy takes the idiosyncratic form $I = S + \bar{D} + \bar{B} + \bar{R} + \bar{F}$ where I is private investment, S is private savings, $\bar{D}$ is autonomous bank credit (for investment purposes), $\bar{B}$ is autonomous interfirm borrowing (for investment purposes, including new flotations in the domestic capital market, $\bar{R}$ is autonomous government subsidy (transfer payments earmarked for selected private investment projects), and $\bar{F}$ is autonomous foreign borrowing (including foreign bank loans and new flotations in foreign capital markets). The corporate component (unspecified here) of S and the whole of $\bar{D}, \bar{B}, \bar{R}$, and $\bar{F}$ all represent investible finances and presuppose the presence of physical resources that could be utilized for the production of capital goods.

   In the future, however, Japan's private investment ratio is likely to decline to a level not much higher than the prevailing private savings ratio, partly because of the inherent instability of other sources of investible funds (especially $\bar{D}, \bar{B}$, etc.), but mainly for the lack of idle physical resource counterparts to be mobilized by those finances. If so, Japan's private investment ratio probably will equal or approximate its private savings ratio: $I/Y \cong S/Y$ instead of $I/Y = S/Y + \bar{D}/Y + \bar{B}/Y + \bar{R}/Y + \bar{F}/Y$. The Japanese economy has thus far enjoyed the advantage of carrying on its private investment activity far beyond what private saving alone would permit, the excess of private investment over private saving in terms of ratios being $I/Y - S/Y = \bar{D}/Y + \bar{B}/Y + \bar{R}/Y + \bar{F}/Y$. The specific reasons for the instability and unreliability of those non-savings sources of investible funds are made clear in a later chapter on monetary-fiscal policies. Suffice it here to suggest that the likelihood of their prevailing ($I/Y \cong S/Y$) will be the greater, the more completely capital and labor are utilized in future, no matter how great the potential finances to mobilize otherwise available idle physical resources may be.

SOCIAL OVERHEAD CAPITAL

   In Japan, social overhead capital formation is virtually synonymous with public investment even if a part of public investment is in plant and equipment (e.g., via the nationalized industries) and even though a part of such capital is formed by the private sector (e.g., private schools and hospitals). Japan's traditional state paternalism and its postwar welfare-statism, coupled with the generally intangible benefits of social overhead capital relative to its obviously heavy costs, render social overhead capital formation particularly congenial to public policymaking.[23] Accordingly, it seems plausible to treat Japan's overhead capital formation as public investment in contradistinction to private investment, as will be so treated in this section. We shall, moreover, concentrate on the cause-and-effect relation between social overhead capital and stable growth in the Japanese economy. My own view of the contributory role of social overhead capital in the growing Japanese economy are rather different from those held by most Japanese economists, for reasons which will be specified.

Social overhead capital generally means that part of the total stock of capital which owes its origin and existence to the public interest at large and which has no direct bearing on the productive process. The pedagogic question of what specific items are to fall in the conceptual category of social overhead capital could be answered variously, depending on the analytical purpose and value judgment of the pedagogue. As a first approximation, we may let it consist of such items as education-welfare facilities (schools, hospitals, etc.), transportation-communications systems (roads, harbors, airports, dams, etc.), land-reclamation facilities, and public buildings, items which are associated with what the Japanese economists call *gyosei toshi* (administrative public investment). With this conceptual context of social overhead capital in mind, let us proceed to the significance and implications of Table 16.

Table 16. Social Overhead vs. Producers' Capital
(as percentage of total capital stock)

Year	Social Overhead Capital*	Producers' Capital**
1946	51.0	48.9
1950	48.5	51.6
1954	45.4	54.6
1957	42.2	57.8

SOURCE: adapted from Nakayama, ed., *Nihon Keizai No Seicho*, p. 28; the figures are based on data from the Economic Planning Agency's 1960 *Sengo Nihon No Keizai Seicho* [The economic growth of postwar Japan] (Tokyo, 1965). No such breakdown figures for later dates are available.
*Includes a privately owned part.
**Includes a publicly owned part.

[23] For the concept of public investment in the postwar Japanese context, see Japanese Economic Planning Agency, *Nihon Keizai No Choki Tenbo* [A long-run view of the Japanese economy] (Tokyo, 1960).

The figures for 1946 in Table 16 reflect the extensive damage inflicted on privately owned plant and equipment during the war and the immediate postwar need for public initiative in the formation of social overhead capital as a general recovery measure. Thereafter the proportion of social overhead capital to postwar Japan's total stock of capital declined progressively, implying greater and greater reliance on private fixed investment for rapid economic recovery and growth. However, we saw from Table 14 that public investment began increasing relative to private investment from 1962 on, implying a reversal of the earlier downward trend of social overhead capital formation soon after the launching of the income-doubling plan in 1961. The Tokyo Olympics in 1964 had the fortuitous effect of furthering social overhead capital formation, especially along the lines of construction of highways and other transportation facilities.[24] Present indications are that the Japanese government will push up the ratio of social overhead capital to the total capital stock, partly because of its public welfare commitments, and partly because of its probable desire to prevent the future danger of excess capacity in the private sector from jeopardizing the stable growth of the economy as a whole.

Perhaps in anticipation of the aforementioned rising trend of social overhead capital formation, in 1960 Dr. O. Shimomura sounded a warning about the risk of increased social overhead capital formation becoming an obstacle to Japan's further economic growth.[25] Dr. Shimomura and other like-minded economists take this position for three reasons. First, they tend to look at social overhead capital formation from the orthodox standpoint of resource allocation and thus the supposedly competitive claim of that capital formation on scarce resources. This reasoning involves the questionable assumption that Japan's total resources will remain constant even in the long run, although new resources may well be discovered, invented, or imported. In view of such dynamic technological and international possibilities, it would be a serious mistake to adhere to the static, conventional idea that social overhead capital cannot be augmented except by limiting the resources available to private capital goods industries.

Second, Dr. Shimomura and some other Japanese economists seem inclined to treat all social overhead capital formation as if it were entirely of the pyramid-building variety with zero marginal productivity, on a par with prewar "military investment." Professor M. Shinohara passively accepts such a view by regarding social overhead capital "as not having any definite relation to capacity."[26] Postwar Japan's constitutional limitation on "military

---

[24] See Federation of Economic Organizations, *Japan Striving for Better Global Co-operation*, p. 17.

[25] See Shimomura's contribution in Nakayama, ed., *Nihon Keizai No Seicho*, especially p. 113.

[26] Shinohara, in *ibid.*, p. 112, n. 2.

investment" is itself a presumption in favor of the contrary view that its social overhead capital is also capable of creating productive capacity. Few would deny that publicly built schools, hospitals, harbors, highways, and other similar components of social overhead capital have greater productivity potential than armaments and other byproducts of pyramid-building investment activity. To exclude social overhead capital as a non-capacity-increasing variable may be statistically expedient, but such an expedience is, in my view, conceptually illegitimate. I shall expand upon this view a little later.

Third, Dr. Shimomura and his Japanese colleagues seem completely indifferent to the demand-generating aspect of social overhead capital formation, as though the Japanese economy at this juncture (compared with the immediate postwar period, with its understandable scarcity of producers' durables) did not need social overhead capital outlays at all as an additional source of aggregate demand, especially for the longer-run purpose of achieving and maintaining stable growth (such as is now emphasized by the Economic Planning Agency). Dr. Shimomura surely is aware of the "dual character" of investment, judging from his fond application of Domar's growth equation, yet he seems to have such implicit faith in the potential sufficiency of private investment and exports as to ignore public social overhead capital outlays that could otherwise be considered helpful in the expansion of effective demand relative to that of productive capacity and hence in achieving stable growth. [27]

More encouraging is Professor S. Ichimura's suggestion that at least a part of social overhead capital formation, i.e., "educational investment," may have been a significant determinant of Japan's historical economic growth.[28] He bases his suggestion on the empirical findings of the Education Ministry's White Paper *Nihon No Seicho To Kyoiku* (Japan's Growth and Education), whereby "educational investment" (measured in terms of outlays per unit of time for school buildings, teachers' salaries, and other educational purposes) is shown to have increased faster than "physical investment" (presumably in plant and equipment) over the 1905–60 period relative to the rising rate of growth of national income. Professor Ichimura draws the inference that therefore Japan's rising rate of growth of national income over that period was led and promoted more by "educational investment" than by "physical investment." However, neither Professor Ichimura nor the Education Ministry provides an operationally significant mechanism to elucidate the cause-and-effect relations involved. This gives me a point of departure for a more constructive and positive discussion of the potential role of social overhead capital in Japan's future economic growth.

[27] I have elsewhere criticized Dr. Shimomura's neglect of the demand side of the growing Japanese economy; see Appendix.

[28] See Ichimura, *Sekai No Nakano Nihon Keizai*, pp. 62–67.

Using the classification of capital given in Table 16 but limiting social overhead capital formation to the specific category of "public investment" involved in Table 14 (government outlays for schools, hospitals, roads, and other durable capital equipment of the non-pyramid-building, non-inventory variety), we have the identity $\Delta K \equiv \Delta K^s + \Delta K^p = I^s + I^p$, where K is the total physical stock of capital, K^s is public social overhead capital, K^p is private producers' capital, I^s is net investment in social overhead capital equipment, and I^p is net investment in producers' capital equipment.

Theoretically, there are two ways in which social overhead capital formation, as such, is capable of affecting the rate of growth of productive capacity, directly, as a co-determinant of output expansion in a given state of technology, and indirectly, as a determinant of the technological parameter affecting capacity expansion. We may see how the process works, as follows: taking the above identity into account, we may let our capacity expansion function take the form $\Delta Y = \sigma(\Delta K^s + \Delta K^p) = \sigma(I^s + I^p)$, where Y is national output or productive capacity and σ is the positive constant marginal productivity of capital in general. Dividing both sides of the equation by Y yields the rate of growth of productive capacity

$$\frac{\Delta Y}{Y} = \sigma\left(\frac{I^s}{Y} + \frac{I^p}{Y}\right)$$

which indicates the possibility that productive capacity may increase faster with a positive public net investment ratio ($I^s/Y > 0$) than with a positive private investment ratio ($I^p/Y > 0$) in a given state of technology ($\sigma = $ a constant). Judging from the rising trend of the public investment ratio in Table 14, we may infer that the Japanese economy's future productive capacity will be helped rather than hindered by the expansion of social overhead capital, especially if that capital takes the form of roads, harbors, airports, or any other instrument of production in a broad sense. To exclude the dynamic role of social overhead capital as if $I^s/Y = 0$ prevailed would be as narrow and unrealistic as the physiocrats' preclassical assumption that only land can have any meaningful relation to "productive" capacity.

Turning now to the second causal channel, we may let the average productivity of capital be given by

$$\sigma \equiv \frac{Y}{K} = \frac{Y}{K^s + K^p} = \frac{\dfrac{Y}{N}}{\dfrac{K^s + K^p}{N}} = \frac{\dfrac{Y}{N}}{\left(\dfrac{K^s}{N}\right) + \left(\dfrac{K^p}{N}\right)} = \frac{\rho}{\Theta_s + \Theta_p},$$

where N is labor input, σ is the average (= marginal on some assumption) productivity of capital, Θ_s is the ratio of social overhead capital to labor, and

Θ_p is the ratio of producers' capital to labor. Here we see, at first blush, the ominous possibility of capital productivity being reduced as a consequence of a rise in the ratio of social overhead capital to labor, inasmuch as σ is shown to vary inversely with K^s/N as well as with K^p/N while varying directly with Y/N. This seems to have misled many Japanese economists into believing that the "productivity coefficient" (σ, in this instance) will probably become smaller with an increase in social overhead capital.[29] What they have overlooked is the interdependence effect of an increase in K^s/N upon Y/N that is not shown explicitly in the above determination of σ. This is where I find it crucially important to make the following additional assumptions explicitly:

$$\frac{\partial(\log \rho)}{\partial(\log \Theta_s)} > 1, \quad \frac{\partial(\log \rho)}{\partial(\log \Theta_p)} = 1,$$

the first of which assumptions is based on the observable fact that a per capita increase in the stock of social overhead capital (especially in the forms of schools, hospitals, and houses) makes for a more intelligent and efficient labor force. A given percentage increase in the ratio of social overhead capital to labor is assumed here to entail a more than proportional increase in the ratio of output to labor, that is, labor productivity on the average and as a whole. The second unitary assumption about the effect of a percentage change in the ratio of producers' capital to labor on labor productivity is made here for the purpose of isolating the role of social overhead capital. However, this latter assumption might not be too unrealistic in the prevailing circumstances in Japan where "20-40 percent of these [small-scale] firms' fixed investment is composed of used machines bought from big firms," according to Professor Shinohara's report.[30] Thus, if increased capital intensity (greater K^p/N, in this case) merely means equipping labor with more physically inefficient secondhand machines, etc., overall labor productivity may not increase significantly in the absence of some offsetting innovations by large-scale firms.

If the productivity of capital (σ) increases, based on the assumptions above about the more than unitary elasticity of labor productivity with respect to social overhead capital intensity, then the rate of growth of productive capacity can be shown to increase over time:

$$\left(\frac{\Delta Y}{Y}\right)_t = \bar{s}\sigma_t = \bar{s}\sigma_0(1 + \epsilon)^t,$$

[29] For a widespread fear of this among economists, see Nakayama, ed., *Nihon Keizai No Seicho.*

[30] See Shinohara, in *ibid.*, p. 208, n. 3.

where ϵ is the rate of increase in the productivity of capital, s is the savings ratio ($s = s_t = \bar{s}$ is assumed), and $\sigma = Y/K = \Delta Y/\Delta K$ (assumed). Here we are substituting the savings ratio for the investment ratio on the tacit assumption that the savings-investment equilibrium condition is satisfied in terms of ratios ($s = S/Y = I^s/Y + I^p/Y$).

Thus it is mainly through the salutary influence of social overhead capital on general labor productivity that the productivity of capital in general can be shown to increase, to the ultimate benefit of capacity expansion. Over and above such a formal demonstration, the intrinsic merit of social overhead capital, so articulately and refreshingly stressed by Professor T. Shibata and his co-authors of *Sumiyoi Nihon*, is clear from the broadest standpoint of social welfare, especially in the context of an ever more affluent Japan.

CHAPTER SIX

LABOR SHORTAGES AS A CRITICAL BOTTLENECK

The Japanese economy, for the first time and with dramatic suddenness, began experiencing a perceptible shortage of labor relative to the growing demand for labor just prior to the 1961 initiation of the income-doubling plan. An acute chronic shortage of labor has since come to be feared as the principal roadblock in expansion of the Japanese economy. The 1965 Economic Planning Agency's White Paper on stable growth reiterates the agency's earlier apprehensions about an impending critical shortage of labor, while Japanese economists continue to debate points of the controversial *rodoryoku fusoku tenkeiron* ("labor shortage transition theory"). All this may come to most Western readers as a surprise, for did they not hear only yesterday of Japan's "overpopulation" and "cheap labor"?[1]

Professor S. Ichimura, after a brief comment on the labor shortage theory, concludes that Japan's medium-range target growth rate of 8.1 percent may be maintained for several years from 1965 on, but that thereafter its declining population growth may well reduce that rate by more than 2 percent.[2] However, he does not go much beyond a suggestive mention of population and automation as basic factors affecting postwar Japan's labor situation, nor do Professor N. Kamakura[3] and others[4] who have made more than casual observations on the subject.

---

[1] Some readers may recall the following Reuters dispatch from Tokyo dated November 10, 1964: "The Japanese people are experiencing a phenomenon almost new to them—a shortage of labor. Except for a brief period during World War II, Japan has suffered from chronic over-population and under-employment for nearly a century. But now, things are changing radically under pressure of massive industrialization. In an effort to attract recruits, large mills and plants are offering higher wages and shorter working hours. Offices and factories are installing equipment and machines to save labor. Demand has been mounting rapidly for electronic computers, teleprinters, and automation systems" (*New York Post*, November 10, 1964).

[2] Ichimura, *Seikai No Nakano Nihon Keizai*, p. 176.

[3] *Nihon Keizairon* [A theory of the Japanese economy] (Tokyo, 1965), p. 35ff.

[4] See the Nakayama symposium on growth; see also T. Ishizaki, "Keiki Choseikano Rodoryoku Fusoku" [The labor shortage under anti-cyclical adjustments], in *Japan Economic Research Center Monthly Report*, September, 1965, p. 11ff.

Accordingly, my specific purpose in this chapter is twofold, to analyze the nature and causes of the prevailing and continuing shortage of labor as the rule rather than the exception in the Japanese economy of today and tomorrow, and to suggest ways and means of alleviating the problem on the basis of the theoretical analysis and empirical observations made. I shall discuss the labor shortage problem under the two broad headings of the macro supply of labor and the macro demand for labor, albeit in the Japanese context.

THE MACRO SUPPLY OF LABOR

For the economy as a whole, we can consider that there is a chronic labor shortage when the total supply of labor as some function of population, etc., is persistently smaller than the total demand for labor as some function of output, etc. As a general frame of reference, therefore, we may express a chronic shortage of labor in the form of an inequality:

$$\frac{\partial(\log N_t{}^s)}{\partial(\log P_t)} - \frac{\partial(\log N_t{}^d)}{\partial(\log Y_t)} < 0,$$

which says that the trend value of the elasticity of the supply of labor with respect to total population is smaller than that of the elasticity of the demand for labor with respect to national output. Here Y is output, P is total population, N^s is the labor input supplied, and N^d is the labor input demanded, while t stands for time. We are interested, for the present, in the first of these terms of the inequality.

Further, we may generalize the supply side of the labor shortage problem in terms of key equations:

(1.1) $N_t{}^s = \eta_t P_t$

(1.2) $P_t = P_0 (1 + \partial)^t$

(1.3) $\eta_t = \eta_0(1 - \lambda)^t$

(1.4) $N_t{}^s = \eta_0 (1 - \lambda)^t P_0 (1 + \partial)^t$

Here the new variables are P_0, representing the initial size of total population; η_0, denoting the initial value of η; η, denoting the ratio of labor to population, or what I call the manpower coefficient (otherwise called "participation ratio"), expressing the community's choice between work and leisure; ∂, representing the constant rate of increase in total population; and λ, representing the constant rate of decrease in the manpower coefficient. From equations (1.1) – (1.3) we get equation (1.4), showing that employable labor (N^s) at time t is co-determined by the dynamic behavior or total population (P_t) and the manpower coefficient (η_t).

The question arises here as to the specific reasons why the Japanese economy should experience a positive but small rate of growth of population and a negative rate of change in the manpower coefficient. The following points might be offered in explanation:

(1) a stronger desire for leisure in the form of shorter working hours, longer vacations with pay, more time for arts and literature, golf, flower arrangements, and other "finer things of life," and *kengaku* ("observation") as well as *kanko* ("sightseeing") trips not only at home but abroad;

(2) pervading birth control practices (including legalized abortion) reinforced by young couples' tendency to prefer a new car to a new baby, as in other highly industrialized areas of the world;

(3) a constantly extended social security program (the present 7 percent ratio of social security benefit payments to national income under Japan's Livelihood Protection Law is still lower than in most Western industrial societies, but it nevertheless guarantees each national a minimum standard of life, a semblance of medical care, modest unemployment compensation, and other welfare benefits), thereby weakening the traditional "hand-to-mouth" motivation to work;

(4) more and longer schooling at all levels (including the new postwar coeducational institutions), keeping a greater number of youths out of the normal labor force than in the past;

(5) the higher average money income of the typical breadwinner in a more and more affluent society, obviating the necessity for supplementary jobs by members of his family (somewhat counterbalanced by higher consumer prices that induce some housewives to seek full-time employment);

(6) rapid urbanization and industrialization, making for a drastic reduction in the agricultural population, hitherto regarded as a permanent and adequate reservoir of employable labor (so much so that Japanese economists are understandably worried about what they call *san-chan-nogyo*, that is, an agrarian economy run by a relatively unproductive trio of a "grandpa," a "grandma," and a "ma," with all the really productive members of the representative rural family permanently migrated to big cities);

(7) a propensity to work less over a high range of real wage rates in the labor market (expressible as a backward-bending supply of labor curve in a macro sense) and in full employment booming conditions.

For these institutional and psychological reasons the application of equation (1.4) to the growing Japanese economy beyond 1970 would, ceteris paribus, yield a chronic shortage of labor—unless the demand for labor could be supposed to decrease for some unforeseen reason. Japan is therefore no exception to the rule that the rate of growth of population in most affluent societies tends to be lowered by the birth rate, which varies inversely with the stock of capital per head, as well as by the death rate, which also varies inversely with the means of consumption per head.[5] Accordingly, the total population and the manpower coefficient in the postwar Japanese economy can be expected to behave in the manners described by equations (1.2) and (1.3).

Let us now turn to some empirical considerations. In Table 17, "employable labor" is a rough version of what the Japanese call *seisan nenrei jinko* ("productive-age population") or the labor force between fifteen and fifty-nine years of age. The estimated rise in the total population from 91.1 million in the 1956-58 base period to 102.2 million in the 1970 target year is quantitatively insignificant, the average annual rate of growth ($\Delta P/P$) being 0.9 percent for the 1956-70 period. Such a low rate of growth of population is itself a presumption against there being sufficient labor to man a growing stock of capital. The manpower coefficient (η) is estimated to fall from 66.8 percent in the 1956-58 period to 61.6 percent in the 1970 target year, giving substance to the hypothesis that the manpower coefficient will change at the negative rate $-\lambda$. The institutional and psychological reasons for the secular trends of population growth and the manpower coefficient indicated in Table 17 were outlined above.

Table 17. Postwar Japan's Population and Manpower

Period	Total Population (P)	Employable Labor (N^S)	Manpower Coefficient ($N^S/P = \eta$)
1956-58 (Base)	91.1 million	65.2 million	66.8%
1970 (Target)	102.2 million	62.9 million	61.6%

SOURCE: adapted from the Economic Planning Agency's 1963 Income-Doubling Plan.

Japanese economists seem unduly pessimistic and fatalistic in their interpretation of empirical data about the supply side of the labor shortage problem, such as is provided in Table 17, partly because they do not tackle the problem simultaneously on the demand front as well, but mainly because they tend to regard the manpower shortage as involving formidable tradition-bound obstacles of an extraeconomic nature. Be that as it may, I propose the following measures to keep up the supply of labor relative to the given demand for labor:

[5] For an alternative approach, see Irene Taeuber, "Population Growth and Economic Development in Japan," *Journal of Economic History*, Fall 1951.

(1) a conscious and bold break with the traditional life-long employment system (*shushin koyosei*) in order to promote greater interfirm labor mobility (not just from small- and medium-sized firms to large firms but from low-paying large firms to high-paying large firms), thus permanently freeing the employer from an unrealistic obligation to keep his employees on the payroll regardless of business cycles and the employee from a moral commitment to remain loyal to his employer indefinitely irrespective of better opportunities elsewhere;

(2) a similar break with the traditional seniority payment system (*nenko joretsugata chingin seido*) in order to increase the incentive to enter the labor force or to remain in it, thus discarding, once and for all, the outmoded personnel policy of raising salaries and wages according to the length of service in favor of a more attractive and equitable system of reward purely on the basis of merit;

(3) the productive reallocation and utilization of the disguised unemployed with zero marginal productivity (e.g., self-employed shopkeepers, street peddlers, seasonal farmhands, and national defense personnel);

(4) the improvement of labor-management relations to prevent prolonged strikes, lockouts, and other wasteful work stoppages, especially in those strategic industries which have far-reaching repercussions on the functioning of the whole economy (if collective bargaining proves ineffective, compulsory arbitration may become necessary);

(5) the greater utilization of female labor not only for conventional services but also for less conventional technical jobs, based on the improvement in educational training for young women since the war and the newly accepted democratic principle of the equality of the sexes;

(6) the strengthening of the existing nation-wide public labor exchange system (*kokyo shokugyo antei sho*) to make the qualified jobseeker available to the right employer at the right time and in the right place (instead of relying upon the existing dubious and often unscrupulous private employment agencies);

(7) systematic job-training programs, public and private, for the so-called "unemployables" (school dropouts, reform-school graduates, hoodlums, alcoholics, narcotics addicts, disabled and handicapped workers, convicts, etc.);

(8) greater flexibility in the enforcement of the retirement age regulation, thereby making it possible for older experienced employees to remain in the labor force beyond the conventional retirement age of sixty (higher in academic circles);

(9) a public policy of encouragement of "imports" of qualified foreign specialists and even unskilled workmen on a purely technical basis (according to the specific domestic needs for their services, and irrespective of national origin, color, or creed), coupled with a national policy of discouragement of "exports" of indigenous experts (mathematicians, econometricians, electronic

technicians, and other Japanese specialists who are disenchanted with low salaries at home and are naturally attracted to better-paying opportunities abroad).

Japanese economists would certainly favor some of these reform possibilities on the supply front, but few of them seem unconventional or unorthodox enough to put forward a program incorporating all of these measures as the basis for a deliberate growth policy. Even if they were to do so, Japanese policymakers might not implement them for political reasons. If economists and policymakers should fail on this score, the growing Japanese economy will be that much the worse even if they proved more willing to tackle the labor shortage problem on the demand front. With this warning, let us now proceed to the demand side of the problem.

THE MACRO DEMAND FOR LABOR

As we did on the supply side, we may generalize the demand side of the labor shortage problem in terms of the following equations for the whole economy:

(2.1) $N_t{}^d = n_t Y_t$

(2.2) $Y_t = Y_0 (1 + g)^t$

(2.3) $n_t = n_0 (1 + \delta)^t$

(2.4) $N_t{}^d = n_0 (1 + \delta)^t Y_0 (1 + g)^t$

Here Y is national output, N^d is the amount of labor input demanded, n is the labor-output ratio (reciprocal of the average productivity of labor), g is the rate of growth of output, δ is the rate of increase in the labor-output ratio, and t is time, while Y_0 and n_0 are, respectively, the initial values of those variables. Here the crucially important equation is (2.3), which shows that the amount of labor input demanded per unit of output ($n = N/Y$) increases exponentially at the constant rate δ. Equation (2.4), which is derived from (2.1) - (2.3), indicates the possibility that the amount of labor demanded by the whole economy increases *pari passu* with the compound growth of output and the labor-output ratio. It is by comparing equations (2.1) - (2.4) representing the demand side with the previous equations (1.1) - (1.4) representing the supply side that we come to understand the precise nature of labor scarcity in a growing economy.

With this in mind, let us look into the empirical aspects of the demand side within the Japanese economy and in relation to other industrial economies. Let us first consider the significance and implications of postwar Japan's changing employment structure, as shown in Table 18. The average annual rate of growth of total employment through 1970 is estimated at 1.2 percent, but this figure becomes interesting and even alarming only when compared

Table 18.   Postwar Japan's Employment Structure

Employment Category*	1955	1960	1963	1956–70 $(\Delta N^d/N^{d**})$
	%	%	%	%
Total employment (N^d)	100.0	100.0	100.0	1.2 $(\Delta N^d/N^d)$
Agriculture $(N_1{}^d/N^d)$	39.6	32.0	27.9	-2.8 $(\Delta N_1{}^d/N_1{}^d)$
Manufacturing $(N_2{}^d/N^d)$	24.4	28.0	31.0	3.5 $(\Delta N_2{}^d/N_2{}^d)$
Service $(N_3{}^d/N^d)$	36.0	40.0	41.1	5.8 $(\Delta N_3{}^d/N_3{}^d)$

SOURCE: adapted from Federation of Economic Organizations, *Economic Picture of Japan*, based on data from Bureau of Statistics, Office of the Prime Minister.

*N^d denotes the size of total employment for the whole economy or the total labor input demanded, $N_1{}^d$, $N_2{}^d$, and $N_3{}^d$ being those of the primary, secondary, and tertiary sectors, respectively.

**$\Delta N^d/N^d$ denotes the average annual rate of change in total employment, $\Delta N_1{}^d/N_1{}^d$, etc., being the sectoral counterparts; the figures for the 1956–70 period are those estimated in the Economic Planning Agency's 1963 Income-Doubling Plan.

with the 1.4 percent rate of growth of the labor force $(\Delta N^s/N^s)$ as estimated through 1970.[6] The intuitively obvious implication of such a comparison is that the growing Japanese economy of tomorrow will have too small a margin of safety in the form of labor reserves to be complacent about the unimpeded process of production. The Economic Planning Agency's estimated figure of 1.2 percent as the average annual rate of growth of employment seems downward-biased in view of the paradoxically more and more labor-intensive structure of the capital-rich Japanese economy, as evidenced by the service category in the table.

Second, the steady decrease in agricultural employment $(N_1{}^d)$ from 1955 on points to a significantly negative rate of change $(\Delta N_1{}^d/N_1{}^d < 0)$ for the 1956–70 period. This drastic decline in the agricultural sector represents the relentless operation of the law of diminishing returns that cannot, because of the geographical and institutional nature of the Japanese case, be readily counterbalanced by technological innovations. As in other advanced industrial economies, the agricultural sector, both as a contributor to total employment and as a supplier of foodstuffs and raw materials, is rapidly becoming a marginal industry which could hardly survive without the government's farm support policy or its protectionist measures against competitive imports.[7]

Third, the increase in the relative contribution of the manufacturing sector to total employment is not at all surprising in the light of the fact that the production index for that sector (1960 = 100) jumped from 48.9 in 1955 to

[6] Economic Planning Agency, Income-Doubling Plan.

[7] For a sympathetic discussion of the agrarian problem from an interindustry point of view, see Ichimura, *Sekai No Nakano Nihon Kezai*, pp. 153, 173–77.

149.5 in 1963.[8] Accordingly, the 3.5 percent rate of growth of manufacturing employment $(\Delta N_2{}^d/N_2{}^d)$ might be regarded as a plausible estimate for the 1956–70 period in view of the 14.3 percent rate of growth of manufacturing output $(\Delta Y^m/Y^m)$ averaged over the 1955–63 period.[9] Whether manufacturing employment will continue to grow at the average rate of 3.5 percent beyond 1970 depends partly on the future intersectoral mobility of labor and partly on the future productivity of labor in the manufacturing sector itself. We shall return to this point in connection with employment elasticity data.

Last, and most significant, the rising trend of employment in the service sector (including transportation, communications, and welfare enterprises that the Economic Planning Agency excludes from the tertiary sector for some reason) over the 1955–63 period, highest of the three sectoral rates shown in the last column of the table, reflects the postwar Japanese structural shift toward the tertiary sector in keeping with the general trend of all advanced industrial societies that require more and better services (especially government services, in keeping with welfare statecraft) as well as goods. However, because of the labor-intensive nature of the case, the service sector as a whole is likely to aggravate the future problem of labor scarcity relative not only to its own requirement of labor input but also to that of the manufacturing sector. This likelihood will be found to have a far-reaching influence upon the speed and pattern of the Japanese economy in the decades ahead.[10]

In Table 19, the elasticity of employment with respect to manufacturing output (e) in each case represents the extent to which the amount of labor input demanded increases in response to a given percentage increment of manufacturing output. We should note that the employment elasticities of all the countries involved are significantly below unity $(e < 1)$, suggesting a generally high productivity of labor in the manufacturing sector of each industrial country. The figure for Japan compares favorably with those for the U.S. and the U.K., but it may not decline to such a low as is represented by Sweden's manufacturing sector unless Japan's productivity of manufacturing labor increases much faster than in the past. It is interesting that West Germany has the highest employment elasticity in spite of its overall rapid economic growth. The relatively low figures for France and Italy seem to reflect comparatively high labor productivities of their manufacturing industries during the 1956–60 period, at any rate.

---

[8] The production indices are those estimated by the Ministry of International Trade and Industry (see Federation of Economic Organizations, *Economic Picture of Japan*, p. 59).

[9] *Ibid.*, p. 5.

[10] Some insight into the interindustry implication of that requirement can be discerned in my policy suggestions at the end of this demand section.

Table 19. *International Employment Elasticities in Manufacturing Industries (1950-60 averages)*

Country	Employment Elasticity: $\partial(\log N_2{}^d)/\partial(\log Y^m) = e$	Productivity Elasticity Ranking: e^{-1}
Sweden	0.09	first
France	0.11	second
Italy	0.13	third
U.S.	0.28	fourth
Japan	0.29	fifth
U.K.	0.31	sixth
West Germany	0.47	seventh

SOURCE: the figures are those calculated by N. Kamakura (*Nihon Keizairon*, p. 36) on the basis of data from UN, *Statistical Yearbook*, and OECD, *General Statistical Bulletin*. He does not specify the productivity elasticity as the reciprocal of the employment elasticity, however.

The concept of employment elasticity is also important for the light it throws on the relative contribution of labor input to output as well as on the relative share of wages in the total income. This is what the productivity elasticity ranking in the table is intended to convey. The productivity elasticity is specified as the reciprocal of the employment elasticity. We may clarify this inverse relation, thus:

$$e = (\Delta N_2{}^d/N_2{}^d)/(\Delta Y^m/Y^m)$$
$$= (Y^m/N_2{}^d)(\Delta N_2{}^d/\Delta Y^m) \sim \partial(\log N_2{}^d)/\partial(\log Y^m);$$
$$e^{-1} = 1/[(\Delta N_2{}^d/N_2{}^d)/(\Delta Y^m/Y^m)]$$
$$= (\Delta Y^m/Y^m)/(\Delta N_2{}^d/N_2{}^d) \sim \partial(\log Y^m)/\partial(\log N_2{}^d).$$

Therefore, to say that the employment elasticity (e) is large is to imply that the elasticity of output with respect to labor input (e^{-1}) is small. What exactly is the relation of this productivity elasticity to the total output of the manufacturing sector? Assume, for the manufacturing sector of any country, the production function of the form

(3.1) $Y^m = f(N_2{}^d, K_2{}^d)$

where Y^m is output, $N_2{}^d$ is labor input, and $K_2{}^d$ is capital input. Following Euler's theorem, we may specify equation (3.1) as

(3.2) $Y^m = \left(\dfrac{\partial Y^m}{\partial N_2{}^d}\right) N_2{}^d + \left(\dfrac{\partial Y^m}{\partial K_2{}^d}\right) K_2{}^d$

dividing by Y^m yields

$$(3.3) \quad 1 = \left(\frac{\partial Y^m}{\partial N_2^d}\right)\left(\frac{N_2^d}{Y^m}\right) + \left(\frac{\partial Y^m}{\partial K_2^d}\right)\left(\frac{K_2^d}{Y^m}\right)$$

$$= \left[\partial(\log Y^m)/\partial(\log N_2^d)\right] + \left[\partial(\log Y^m)/\partial(\log K_2^d)\right]$$

$$= \epsilon_n + \epsilon_k$$

Here ϵ_n $(= e^{-1})$ is the elasticity of output with respect to labor input and ϵ_k is the elasticity of output with respect to capital input. From (3.1) and (3.2) we have assumed a linear homogeneous production function in the form given by (3.3), which expresses the typical case of constant returns to scale $(\epsilon_n + \epsilon_k = 1)$. In this connection, the reader will readily recall that such elasticity terms enter the well-known Cobb-Douglas production function as exponents, that is, $Y = aN^\gamma K^{1-\gamma}$ for the whole economy (where a and γ are empirically observed constants). In our special case, however, the assumption of constant returns to scale involved in equation (3.3) is irrelevant, for the main point here is that the relative contribution of manufacturing labor input to total output is clearly shown in terms of the elasticity coefficient ϵ_n $(= e^{-1})$ irrespective of what the elasticity of output with respect to capital input ϵ_k might be. Indeed, if the manufacturing sector desires increasing returns to scale $(\epsilon_n + \epsilon_k > 1)$, it should, for one thing, attempt to increase labor's contribution in terms of its productivity elasticity (ϵ_n) or, what amounts to the same thing, decrease the implied employment elasticity (e):

$$(3.4) \quad \epsilon_n(t) + \epsilon_k(t) > 1 \text{ via } \Delta e^{-1}(t) = \Delta\epsilon_n(t) > 0$$

even if $\Delta\epsilon_k(t) = 0$. Thus viewed, the ranking of the productivity elasticity in the last column of Table 19 becomes operationally significant, especially for the Japanese economy, confronted with an increasing shortage of labor.

Let us now turn to the other implication for the relative share of wages in the total income. Applying Professor S. Weintraub's technique,[11] we may let the ratio of wages to the manufacturing sector's total income be given by

$$(3.5) \quad W^m/Y^m = (\Delta Y^m/\Delta N_2^d)/(Y^m/N_2^d)$$

which shows that the share of real wages in the manufacturing sector's total real income (W^m/Y^m) is equal to the ratio of the marginal physical productivity $(\Delta Y^m/\Delta N_2^d)$ to the average physical productivity of labor (Y^m/N_2^d) or to the "M-A ratio" (in Weintraub's terminology). But then we know that

[11] Weintraub, *An Approach to the Theory of Income Distribution* (Philadelphia, 1958).

the latter ratio is nothing else than the elasticity of output with respect to labor input:

$$(3.6) \quad (\Delta Y^m / \Delta N_2{}^d)/(Y^m / N_2{}^d) = (\Delta Y^m / Y^m)/(\Delta N_2{}^d / N_2{}^d)$$
$$\cong \partial(\log Y^m)/\partial(\log N_2{}^d) = \epsilon_n = e^{-1}$$

Thus we can see that the productivity elasticity ranking in the last column of Table 19 also implies the ranking of the wage-distribution ratios in the manufacturing sectors of the countries concerned. Japan's rank, for instance, can be taken to mean that its manufacturing sector has yet to catch up with the "efficiency-wage" standards (determined by the productivity elasticity via equation [3.5]) of Sweden, France, Italy, and the U.S., that is, in the absence of trade union or government interference with labor markets. I would recommend to Japanese economists further explorations and applications of equations (3.1) – (3.6) in their future theoretical-empirical investigations of the demand side of the labor shortage problem.

Finally, to facilitate further research, I suggest the following broad policy measures to keep down the excessive demand for labor relative to its given supply in conditions of full employment:

(1) greater automation of manufacturing industries, especially those large firms which can easily justify installation of new and better labor-saving devices on grounds of general cost advantage, within technical limits;

(2) managerial integration of overlapping, overcompetitive, overmanned retail stores into the self-service type of supermarket or department store enterprise within the framework of the prevailing anti-trust law;

(3) computerization of all those services which now rely on the conventional, laborious techniques of accounting and researching (e.g., cash registers instead of abacuses, photoduplicating instead of mimeograph machines, computer centers instead of departmentalized calculating machines, etc.);

(4) reduction of bureaucratic overstaffing (e.g., a superfluous "make-work" hierarchy of a president, vice-presidents, assistant vice-presidents, section chiefs, subsection chiefs, etc., all presumably requiring secretaries, typists, porters, and other personal attendants) in government agencies and private business;

(5) greater productivity of service industries as a whole, especially those lending themselves to push-button modernization (e.g., transportation and communications services), in view of the increasing structural shift of employment to the tertiary sector of the economy;

(6) greater mechanization of agricultural production, the well-known geographical and social limitations notwithstanding, wherever and whenever a tractor can be substituted for a horse-drawn plow, a threshing machine for a

hand-operated winnow, a truck for a buggy, a bulldozer for a shovel, a reaping machine for a sickle, etc.;

(7) greater elasticity of substitution of capital for labor in a micro sense via the less oligopolistic downward rigidity of the average price of capital input (g) relative to the given wage rate (w), that is, $[d(\log K^d/N^d)/d(\log q/w)] > 1$, where K^d is the amount of capital input demanded, N^d is labor input demanded, q is the average price of capital input, and w is the average real wage rate);

(8) elimination of oligopsonistic employers' power to keep the average wage rate lower than a competitive level, in accordance with the familiar competitive factor demand law $w = \partial Y/\partial N^d$ instead of the oligopsonistic formula $w < \partial Y/\partial N^d$, on the basis of the inelastic supply of labor curve confronting the oligopsonist (fewer alternative employers to turn to), and with a view to preventing labor input from becoming unduly cheap relative to other inputs and so making the substitution of other inputs for labor more attractive in terms of costs.

In a nutshell, this is what ought to be done on the demand front if the shortage of labor is not to prove an insurmountable obstacle to Japanese economic growth.

CHAPTER SEVEN

THE FISCAL-MONETARY MILIEU
FOR RAPID GROWTH

Postwar Japan seems to me to be a rather unique instance of a modern mixed public-private economy that has vigorously and massively availed itself of the Keynesian concept of functional finance and the Schumpeterian concept of developmental credit for the purposes of national stability and growth. This chapter is intended to provide a structural analysis of the causal relation of postwar Japan's fiscal-monetary setup and its rapid economic growth.[1] The analysis will be made under the conceptually distinct headings of the fiscal milieu and the monetary milieu, even though fiscal and monetary practices are inseparable in the Japanese economy. I shall touch upon what Japanese economists call the "overloan controversy" and shall also suggest some fiscal-monetary reforms to be carried out for a future welfare-oriented pattern of growth.

THE FISCAL MILIEU

International data serve as a useful starting point. During the two fairly comparable periods covered, government expenditures of all the countries

---

[1] For alternative views and interpretations, see the 1966 Iwanami symposium *Nihon Keizai Wa Do Naruka?* [What will become of the Japanese economy?], involving Professors H. Ohuchi, H. Arisawa, Y. Wakimura, R. Minobe, and K. Naito, esp. chaps. 3 and 4; Y. Hayashi, "Capital Accumulation and Taxation in Japan," *National Tax Journal*, June 1963; Y. Hayashi and Y. Shima, eds., *Zaisei Seisaku No Riron* [Theory of fiscal policy] (Tokyo, 1964); K. Emi, *Government Fiscal Activity and Economic Growth in Japan, 1868-1960* (Tokyo, 1963); O. Shimomura, "Keizai Seisaku No Ninmu To Sekinin" [The task and responsibility of economic policy], in *Japan Economic Research Center Monthly Report*, September 1965; M. Bronfenbrenner and K. Kogiku, "The Aftermath of the Shoup Tax Reforms," *National Tax Journal*, September and December 1957; H. Rosovsky, "Capital Formation in Pre-War Japan: Current Findings and Future Problems," in C. D. Cowan, ed., *The Economic Development of China and Japan* (London, 1964); H. T. Patrick, "Cyclical Instability and Fiscal-Monetary Policy in Postwar Japan," in W. W. Lockwood, ed., *The State and Economic Enterprise in Japan* (Princeton, N.J., 1965); Kamakura, *Nihon Keizairon* (esp. chaps. 5, 6, and 7); T. Eguchi, "Keizai Seicho To Tsuika Shinyo" [Economic growth and ancillary credit], in *Keizai Orai* [Economic Comings and Goings], June 1966; Federation of Economic Organizations, *Economic Picture of Japan* (esp. chap. 4, "Public Finance and Financial Institutions of Japan"); OECD, *Economic Surveys: Japan* (Tokyo, 1964) esp. chap. 4.

included grew faster than their GNP. This fact is perhaps a reflection of the growth-welfare age, as well as of expanding mixed public-private economic statecraft. It is noteworthy that the three fast-growing countries Japan, France, and West Germany increased their government expenditures at higher rates than did the United Kingdom and the United States, indicating the former group's primarily growth-oriented government expenditure policy and the latter group's principally welfare-oriented government expenditure policy. This welfare vs. growth orientation is especially marked in the comparison of British and Japanese "transfers and subsidies" (which represent the welfare component of total government expenditure, especially in the U.K.).[2] Be that as it may, the most noteworthy aspect of Table 20 is that both Japan's government expenditure and its real GNP in the postwar period have surpassed those of the other industrial countries.

Table 20. International Rates of Growth of Government Expenditure and Real GNP

Country	Government Expenditure (1954–65)	Real GNP (1955–62)
	%	%
Japan	12.5	10.3
France	8.7	5.0
West Germany	8.2	6.7
U.K.	6.4	2.3
U.S.	4.1	3.5

SOURCE: expenditure data were adapted from the Iwanami symposium, *Nihon Keizai Wa Do Naruka?*, p. 103 (data based on *Analyst*, June 1965). Real GNP figures were adapted from Federation of Economic Organizations, *Economic Picture of Japan*, p. 2 (data based on Bank of Japan, *Statistics for International Comparison*).

Let me now delineate the distinctive features of postwar Japan's government expenditure structure, putting aside its revenue structure for the moment.

1. The most important single feature of postwar Japan's government expenditure structure is the virtual absence of military outlays, which occupied nearly 50 percent of the average prewar total in Japan and which account for more than 50 percent of the postwar total in the United States

[2] For British "transfers and subsidies" see A. T. Peacock and J. Wiseman, *The Growth of Public Expenditure in the United Kingdom* (Princeton, N.J., 1961). For Japanese counterparts see Emi, *Government Fiscal Activity and Economic Growth in Japan*. After making a statistical comparison, Professor Emi observes: "in the increases in transfers and subsidies since 1900, the United Kingdom led Japan all the way from the prewar period up to recent years" (*ibid.*, p. 43).

and other world powers. A far greater proportion of any given annual public revenue can thus be expended on non-military growth-welfare projects than before World War II or in any militarized industrial country, and there is a further implication that the stability of the postwar Japanese economy need no longer depend on so precarious and fortuitous a prop as income-generating but non-capacity-increasing military outlays. Moreover, the traditional pressure for the deficit financing of wars and military adventures at the risk of a ruinous inflation and an alarming public debt is thereby removed permanently, to the long-run advantage of savers, taxpayers, and all others concerned. Thus I agree with Professor Emi, who observes that "the most remarkable difference between the two stages appears as a large reduction in defense expenditure, i.e., from 43.8 percent (in 1900) to 5.2 percent (in 1960)."[3]

2. Another distinctive aspect of postwar Japan's government expenditure structure is the increasing weight of tax-independent "special accounts" which are discretionary (not accountable to the Parliament, in contradistinction to "general accounts" that are tax-financed and subject to parliamentary constraint). The special account of Japan's national budget had increased to 65.7 percent by 1960 (the remainder representing the general account), whereas it amounted to only 34.6 percent of the total in 1900.[4] What exactly is the relevance of this special account to postwar Japan's economic growth? First of all, the outlays involved, e.g., those for foodstuff control (farm subsidies), road construction, public works, land conservation, the fiscal investments and loans program, etc., must be specified. It is the last-named item that is most relevant to rapid economic growth, for under this program, the national government is completely free to utilize non-tax revenues (including domestic and foreign bank loans) for financing the investment projects of government agencies (central and local) as well as those of selected private enterprises (via grants and aids and often interest-free loans). Since special accounts are independent of tax revenues, their growth reflects the expanding role of government activity in the overall spending stream of the postwar Japanese economy unhindered by conventional revenue considerations.

3. Postwar Japan's government expenditure structure has come to be influenced by the capital account to the extent of nearly one-half of the total (43.1 percent for 1946-50, 43 percent for 1951-55, and 45 percent for 1956-60),[5] whereas the prewar government expenditure structure (especially during the Great Depression of the 1930s) was dominated by the current account, representing more than four-fifths of the total. What is more, postwar Japan's government capital expenditures are exclusive of merely

[3] *Ibid.*, p. 61.
[4] *Ibid.*, p. 85.
[5] Calculated from Table 5 in *ibid.*, p. 46.

demand-generating military investment. Thus, in addition to its modern role as a stabilizer (via the multiplier effect of current government expenditure: $\Delta Y^d = k\Delta I^g$, where Y^d is effective demand, I^g is government investment demand, and k is the multiplier), the government has acquired the new and increasingly important role of an investor in fixed capital (including social overheads) or a capacity-creator (via $\Delta Y^s = \sigma I^g = \sigma \Delta K^g$, where Y^s is productive capacity, K^g is government capital stock, I^g is government net investment in durable capital, and σ the productivity of capital). It is interesting to note that other advanced market economies with negligible government investment simply preclude the functional category of the capital account from their government expenditure budgeting, thereby limiting the government's spending role to the current account.[6]

4. Another characteristic of postwar Japan's government expenditure structure is the upward flexibility of transfers and subsidies, as compared with their relative stability in other countries.[7] Total government transfers and subsidies jumped from ¥154.9 billion in 1950 to ¥592.8 billion in 1960, according to the Economic Planning Agency's 1962 White Paper. It is noteworthy that, of the postwar total of transfers and subsidies, 70 percent was allocated to agriculture (presumably under the farm support program), 20 percent to industry, and 10 percent to households.[8] This implies that the government's fiscal aid to industry mainly takes the form of loans (under the fiscal investments and loans program) and tax remissions (to be discussed on the revenue side). The expectations are that the share of households in the total government transfers and subsidies will increase as time goes on, especially in connection with the enlargement of social security programs (national and local). An increase in the relative share of transfers and subsidies going to households would have the effect of increasing the investment multiplier $\{k = 1/[1 - c'(1 - z + r)]\}$ through the increasing impact of larger r on the marginal propensity to consume out of disposable income, c', that is, via $\Delta C = c'(\Delta Y - \Delta T + \Delta R)$ and $\Delta C/\Delta Y = c(1 - z + r)$, where Y is effective demand, T is taxes, R is "transfers and subsidies" to households, C is consumption demand, k is the investment multiplier, c' is the marginal propensity to consume out of disposable income, z is the marginal propensity to tax, and r is the marginal propensity to make transfer payments. I have elsewhere discussed the role of subsidy-financed

---

[6] Compare UN, *A Manual for Economic and Functional Classification of Government Transactions* (New York, 1958); Y. Kato, "Seifuyosan To Kokuminkeizaiyosan" [Government budgeting and national economy budgeting], in Hayashi and Shima, eds., *Zaisei Seisaku No Riron.*

[7] See, e.g., the stable behavior of the British counterpart, in Peacock and Wiseman, *The Growth of Public Expenditure in the United Kingdom.*

[8] Emi, *Government Fiscal Activity and Economic Growth in Japan,* pp. 67, 77.

private investment in economic growth[9] and will not expand upon the point here.

5. Expectational "pump-priming" has become a permanent feature of postwar Japan's government expenditure structure. It is based on the assumption that current private investment is an increasing function of anticipatory national income, an assumption that is reinforced by the traditional sensibilities of the private sector toward state paternalism. We may illustrate the dynamic process of expectational pump-priming thus:

$$(1.1) \quad \Delta I_t{}^P = v\Delta Y^d_{t+1} \quad (v > 0)$$

$$(1.2) \quad \Delta Y^d_{t+1} = k_g \Delta G_{t+1} \quad [k_g = 1/(s + z - v)]$$

$$(1.3) \quad \Delta I_t{}^P = v(k_g \Delta G_{t+1})$$

Here Y^d is effective demand, I^P is private investment, G is government expenditure, v is the positive constant marginal propensity to invest, k_g is the government expenditure multiplier, s is the constant marginal propensity to save, z is the marginal propensity to tax in general, t is the current period, and $t + 1$ is the next period. Equation (1.3), which is derived from equations (1.1) and (1.2), shows the possibility of an increase in private investment demand in the current period $(I_t{}^P)$ in anticipation of government-induced income expansion $(k_g \Delta G_{t+1})$ that is deliberately projected for the next period. Dr. O. Shimomura made a relevant comment on this process during the recession year of 1965: "The announcement that government expenditure will not be reduced (to be sustained via deficit financing, if necessary) serves to avert a further downswing of private economic activity."[10] Indeed, the Japanese government is able to make the advance announcement of its intended outlays (G_{t+1}) in order to stimulate current private investment $(I_t{}^P)$ via the mechanism described by (1.1)–(1.3), and on the budgetary basis of discretionary, tax-independent special accounts.

6. The last distinctive feature of postwar Japan's government expenditure structure is the inflation bias and voter orientation of the fiscal authority. The unorthodox equanimity with which the Japanese fiscal authority dismisses the dangers of excessive government spending in conditions of full employment stands in sharp contrast with the orthodox prudence of even vote-conscious policymakers in other countries. A cutback in government expenditure as a possible anti-inflation weapon is simply considered bad politics, irrespective of what intrinsic economic merits it might have. Thus the government expenditure multiplier mechanism is not readily reversible in

---

[9] See my "A Linear Programming Fiscal-Policy Model of Capacity Growth," *Public Finance*, 20 (1965).

[10] Shimomura, "Keizai Seisaku No Ninmu To Sekinin."

Japan when output is inelastic with respect to effective demand in conditions of full employment. In other words, for political reasons postwar Japan cannot rely upon $-\Delta Y_m = k_p(-\Delta G_m)$, where Y_m is national money income, G_m is governmental money expenditure, and k_p is the price multiplier given by the reciprocal of the constant marginal propensities to save, to tax, and to import out of national money income; $k_p = 1/(a_m + \beta_m + \gamma_m)$, where $a_m = \Delta S_m/(\Delta p)\overline{Y}_f$, $\beta_m = \Delta T_m/(\Delta p)\overline{Y}_f$ and $\gamma_m = \Delta M_m/(\Delta p)\overline{Y}_f$, with Y_f and p denoting constant full employment real income and the general price index, respectively. Professor H. Ohuchi makes an understandably acid criticism of the postwar Japanese fiscal-monetary authorities (especially the Ministry of Finance and the Bank of Japan): "They couldn't care less whether the Japanese people's prices increase and the purchasing power of the consumer yen decreases, so long as the economy's plant and equipment expand. For the sake of private enterprise profits, price hikes are 'inevitable'; inflation is 'unavoidable.' This is the ideology of Japan's finance!"[11] Directing his criticism at Dr. Shimomura, Professor M. Bronfenbrenner has made this tongue-in-cheek comment from the other side of the Pacific: "one of the most original and arresting features of Shimomura's thought is a theory of inflation which has led him to regard with unconcern increases in consumer prices," that is, so long as the stability of wholesale and hence export prices is maintained.[12] I shall reserve my own comments for a later chapter on inflation.

Let us now turn to postwar Japan's tax structure. As on the expenditure side, I shall delineate the distinctive features of the revenue side.

1. The most important distinctive feature of postwar Japan's tax structure is the inordinate weight given to indirect taxes (sales, excise, etc.) affecting the consuming public in general and wage-earners in particular. In 1964,[13] the Ministry of Finance estimated indirect taxes at 41.3 percent of the total, 58.7 percent being the estimated figure for direct taxes (on personal and corporate income). Such excessive reliance on indirect taxes of a regressive nature offsets the effect of progressive income taxes, which affect high-income earners adversely. Inasmuch as persons with high incomes show high propensities to save and to invest, the presumption is that Japan's relatively regressive tax structure is conducive to its rapid economic growth. It appears that the Japanese economy has sacrificed the "ability to pay" democratic-welfare principle of taxation for the sake of rapid growth, contrary to the Shoup tax mission's intentions. Professor H. C. Wallich makes this relevant observation:

---

[11] Iwanami symposium, *Nihon Keizai Wa Do Naruka?*, p. 65; translated from the Japanese original.

[12] Bronfenbrenner, "Economic Miracles and Japan's Income-Doubling Plan," in Lockwood, ed., *The State and Economic Enterprise in Japan.*

[13] See Federation of Economic Organizations, *Economic Picture of Japan*, p. 51.

The industrial countries which have recently enjoyed the fastest economic growth are among those that rely much more on sales and similar taxes than on income taxes. This is strikingly true ... of the European top-growth countries (France, Italy and Germany) as well as of Japan. ... No country can grow rapidly unless it plows back a high proportion of its output into productive investment. High income taxes probably tend to reduce the supply of savings that are needed, because they weigh most heavily on high-income earners who do the most saving. They may also undermine the incentive to invest, as well as the urge to work and make money.[14]

This seemingly unconventional thought is actually more familiar than it may appear at first. Not only pre-Keynesian but classical economists (with the notable exception of Malthus and Marx) tacitly advocated income inequality and the resultant "abstinence of the rich" as the *sine qua non* of economic progress. Professor Wallich may be right as far as the capital-scarce stage of economic development is concerned, but I differ with him in thinking that, at least theoretically, the productivity of capital could be increased for the sake of rapid growth, as a possible alternative to relying on the "abstinence of the rich" sort of taxation to obtain the high savings ratio required. This criticism applies to the Japanese fiscal authorities as well. Since neither they nor Professor Wallich have demonstrated the functional relationship between an implied regressive tax structure and rapid economic growth, let me digress here in order to build the following illustrative model:

(2.1) $z_c = T_c/C^m = T_c/(C_1{}^m + C_2{}^m)$

(2.2) $p_c' = p_c'(t) = p_c(0) + z_c(t); \quad p_c' > p_c \quad [p_c(0) = 1.00]$

(2.3) $C_1'^r = C_1{}^m/p_c', \; C_1{}^r = C_1{}^m/p_c$

(2.4) $C_2'^r = C_2{}^m/p_c', \; C_2{}^r = C_2{}^m/p_c$

(2.5) $C_1'^r = c_1'Y_1, \; C_1{}^r = c_1 Y_1 \quad \left(c_1' = \dfrac{\Delta C_1{}^m/p_c'}{\Delta Y_1}, \; c_1 = \dfrac{\Delta C_1{}^m/p_c}{\Delta Y_1} \right)$

(2.6) $C_2'^r = c_2'Y_2, \; C_2{}^r = c_2 Y_2 \quad \left(c_2' = \dfrac{\Delta C_2{}^m/p_c'}{\Delta Y_2}, \; c_2 = \dfrac{\Delta C_2{}^m/p_c}{\Delta Y_2} \right)$

(2.7) $\eta_1 = \dfrac{c_1 - c_1'}{c_1} = 1 - \dfrac{c_1'}{c_1}$

(2.8) $\eta_2 = \dfrac{c_2 - c_2'}{c_2} = 1 - \dfrac{c_2'}{c_2}$

[14] "For Fastest Growth—What Kind of Tax?," *New York Times Magazine*, September 9, 1962.

(2.9) $Y_1/Y = d,\ Y_2/Y = 1 - d$

(2.10) $C = c_1' Y_1 + c_2' Y_2 = c_1' dY + c_2'(1 - d)Y$

(2.11) $c \equiv C/Y = c_1'^d + c_2'(1 - d),$

(2.12) $g \equiv \dfrac{\Delta Y}{Y} = \dfrac{s}{b} = \dfrac{1 - [c_1'^d + c_2'(1 - d)]}{b}$

Here Y is national output or real income, Y_1 is that part of real income going to low-income brackets as a group, Y_2 is that going to high-income brackets as a group, T_c is sales and similar indirect taxes on all consumer goods in question (presumably passed on to the buyer in toto), C is real consumption for the whole economy, $C_1{}^r$ is real consumption of low-income brackets before tax, $C_2{}^r$ is real consumption of high-income brackets before tax, $C_1'{}^r$ is real consumption of low-income brackets after tax, $C_2'{}^r$ is real consumption of high-income brackets after tax, $C_1{}^m$ is money consumption of low-income brackets, $C_2{}^m$ is money consumption of high-income brackets; z_c is the uniform consumption tax rate (i.e., regressive in tax burden), g is the average annual rate of growth of real income or productive capacity for the whole economy, p_c' is the index of consumer prices after tax, p_c is the index of consumer prices before tax ($p_c = 1.00$ when $z_c = 0$ in the base period), s is the savings ratio for the whole economy, b is the capital coefficient, c is the consumption ratio for the whole economy (average propensity to consume, which is the inverse of s, that is, $1 - s = c;\ s + c = 1$), c_1' is marginal propensity to consume of low-income brackets in real terms after tax, c_2' is marginal propensity to consume of high-income brackets in real terms after tax, c_2 is marginal propensity to consume of low-income brackets before tax, c_2 is marginal propensity to consume of high-income brackets before tax, d is the ratio of low income to national income, $1 - d$ is that of high income to national income, η_1 is the index of tax burden on low-income consumers, η_2 is that on high-income consumers, and t is time ($t = 0, 1$).

This is a simplified model constructed by abstracting from direct taxes, government expenditure, and foreign trade terms, with a view to isolating the presently relevant role of indirect taxes in rapid growth. Equation (2.1) expresses the consumption tax rate as the ratio of such taxes to money consumption made up of low-income and high-income consumption outlays in money terms; here it is tacitly assumed that low-income brackets do the most consuming, which implies that high-income brackets do the most saving. Equation (2.2) makes the tax rate additive to the base period index of consumer prices [if $p_c(0) = 1.00$, $z_c(t) = 0.10$, then $p_c' = 1.10$ after tax]; the tax-included price index is larger than the base period price without the tax, $p_c' - p_c > 0$. Equation (2.3) defines low-income brackets' real consumption before and after tax by deflating their money consumption by the non-tax-included and tax-included price indices, respectively; it is to be noted here that real consumption of low-income brackets is greatly reduced in absolute terms by the numerator $C_1{}^m$ being of large magnitude relative to the denominator p_c'. Equation (2.4) likewise defines high-income brackets' real consumption before and after tax. Equations (2.5) and (2.6) express the real consumption functions of the two income groups before and after tax, with the prime denoting each variable in terms of the tax influence involved; the marginal consumption ratios in parentheses are those before and after tax, with p_c and p_c' serving as deflators and with the tax-influenced c_s' lagging behind the non-tax-influenced ones $(c_1' < c_1,\ c_2' < c_2)$.

Equations (2.7) and (2.8) measure the tax burden of low-income consumers and that of high-income consumers, respectively; the former burden is heavier than the latter because c_1' (after tax) is reduced from c_1 (before tax) by a far larger absolute amount than c_2' (after tax), as the indicators of (2.5) and (2.6) imply. In both cases, $c_1' = c_1$ and $c_2' = c_2$ as in the base period before tax, so that obviously there is no tax burden at all, or $\eta_1,\ \eta_2 = 0$. Equation (2.9) gives the income distribution ratios of the two groups for the purpose of transforming the two consumption functions into the overall consumption ratio for the whole economy (the possible manipulation of d and $1 - d$ through redistributive government expenditure measures is ignored here for simplicity). Equation (2.10) shows total real consumption as the sum of the tax-affected consumption outlays of the two income groups, while (2.11) gives the national consumption ratio derived from (2.9) and (2.10). Finally, making use of the familiar Harrod-Domar growth equation, we have the rate of growth of productive capacity given by (2.12)–a growth rate that incorporates the tax-affected consumption ratios (c_1', c_2'). Equation (2.12) demonstrates the theoretical possibility of an increase in the growth rate (g) as a consequence of the depressing impact of indirect taxes on the real consumption of low-income earners who do the most consuming [expressible as $\Delta c_1'(t) < 0$] and hence of the conversely increased savings in terms of ratios $[\Delta s(t) > 0]$, given the constant capital coefficient $[\Delta b(t) = 0]$ and the constant distribution ratio $[\Delta d(t) = 0]$.[15]

2. Another distinctive feature of postwar Japan's tax structure is a series of tax exemptions for the benefit of investors and savers.[16] They include the

---

[15] This conclusion is no doubt unpalatable to "Underconsumptionists," but I would remind them of the long-run counsel of Keynes, who was a bit of underconsumptionist himself: "All kinds of social customs and economic practices, affecting the distribution of wealth and of economic rewards and penalties, which we now maintain at all costs, however distasteful and unjust they may be in themselves, because they are tremendously useful in promoting the accumulation of capital, we shall then be free, at last, to discard" (*Essays in Persuasion*, pp. 369-70). The time to discard them (including regressive indirect taxes as a stimulant to rapid growth) may come sooner than Professor Wallich or the Japanese fiscal authorities seem to imagine, as far as increasingly affluent societies are concerned.

[16] For details see Hayashi, "Capital Accumulation and Taxation in Japan," and S. Mizuno, "Zaisei To Keizai Seicho" [Public finance and economic growth], in Hayashi and Shima, eds., *Zaisei Seisaku No Riron*.

following: an exemption of taxes on intercorporate dividends (the only Shoup tax reform retained after the 1951 peace treaty, it was originally intended to encourage interfirm borrowing via the capital market but subsequently proved to facilitate borrowing from banks, which do the most intercorporate shareholding); an exemption of taxes, for a specified period, on the income from the sale of officially designated "important products" (e.g., coal, chemical fertilizers, pharmaceutical products, synthetic fibers, and electrical products—in sum, the Schumpeterian category of "new products" deemed vital to economic growth); and an exemption of taxes on capital gains and interest earnings (thus encouraging the amassing of money capital by financial investors through stock market speculation, as well as by rentier savers). These exemptions are reinforced by generous tax deductions, specified below.

3. Another distinctive feature on the revenue side is a series of selective tax deductions for large firms which do the most investing.[17] These deductions are as follows: a liberal scheme of accelerated depreciation[18] (e.g., permitting an initial depreciation allowance in the first year, as high as 50 percent of the original value of a fixed asset, the remaining cost of the asset presumably being written off in equal annual installments till the end of its useful life, thereby encouraging investment in fixed capital); a generous deducation on special reserves of corporations, that part of corporate profits retained in anticipation of losses and expenses (e.g., a bad debt reserve, a price fluctuation reserve, a retirement allowance reserve, and an extraordinary loss reserve); specified deductions from the taxable income of exporting firms (e.g., from 3 percent of export sales to 80 percent of net income); and prescribed percentage deductions from the taxable income of firms paying out dividends on new shares that are floated to raise capital for expansion (another stimulant to "indirect financing" of investment, ostensibly via the capital market but actually via the banking system, which absorbs most of the new flotations). These tax remissions are really indirect subsidies to firms that are large enough to have quantitatively significant taxable incomes and so can take advantage of those tax-relief measures.

4. The last feature of postwar Japan's public revenue structure is the use of unorthodox methods of raising funds for budgetary purposes.[19] These methods are the following: increasing tax revenues by helping to expand the national income, of which income taxes are an increasing function $(dT^y/dY > 0)$, even through inflationary public investment activity and

---

[17]Ibid.

[18]For general discussions, see E. D. Domar, "The Case for Accelerated Depreciation," Quarterly Journal of Economics, November 1953; and my "Capital Theory, Corporate Taxation, and Capacity Expansion," Kyklos, 19 (1966).

[19]For details see Y. Hayashi, Sengo Nihon No Sozei Kozo [The tax structure of postwar Japan] (Tokyo, 1958).

transfers and subsidies to the private sector; budgetary overestimation of the elasticity of taxes with respect to the next fiscal year's national income $[\partial(\log T^y_{t+1})/\partial(\log Y_{t+1}) > 1]$ in order to make advance procurements for private firms under the investments and loans program in the current fiscal year; letting the nationalized industries (e.g., the Railways Corporation, the Telegraph and Telephone Corporation, the Japan Development Bank, and the Export and Import Bank) issue their own debentures to raise capital for expansion; acquiring non-tax revenues and funds from the sale of long-term government securities and foreign exchange to the Central Bank, from postal savings and postal insurance premium payments, and from foreign borrowing (e.g., the World Bank) to meet expenditure needs on special accounts; and acquiring sizable non-tax revenues from the sale of government monopoly products (especially tobacco and cigarettes) for potential use on capital accounts. As a consequence, postwar Japan has enjoyed a rather persistent budgetary surplus on current accounts, while unhesitatingly sustaining a periodic deficit on capital accounts for rapid growth.

THE MONETARY MILIEU

This section will deal with the credit structure, the sources of investible funds, monetary mechanisms for growth, the "overloan" controversy, and other related matters. It may be useful to begin with a brief description of postwar Japan's credit structure. The financial hierarchy of postwar Japan consists of the Bank of Japan at the top, large metropolitan commercial banks (Mitui, Mitsubishi, etc.) with branches all over the country,[20] provincial commercial banks, government credit institutions (Japan Development Bank, Export-Import Bank, etc.), and small private finance companies and cooperatives at the bottom. The Bank of Japan is owned and operated by the national government, and it serves both as the bank of banks and as the central treasurer for the Ministry of Finance and other government agencies. The Bank of Japan is analogous in nature and function to the U.S. Federal Reserve System; it represents the central monetary authority and is empowered to issue notes, to extend credit to government agencies and private banks, to control the total supply of credit (via reserve requirements, rediscount policies, open market operations, and moral suasion) in accordance with broad predetermined national objectives, and to deal with foreign central banks.

Unlike the U.S. Federal Reserve System (which is partly owned by private member banks), the Bank of Japan (which is wholly nationalized, as in England and France) does not adhere to the traditional principle of monetary

---

[20] See K. Suzuki, "Behavior and Profitability of Banking Activities in Postwar Japan: Metropolitan Banks as a Central Force" (in Japanese), *Riron Keizaigaku* [Economic Studies Quarterly], September 1963.

autonomy (independence from political influences, for better or for worse) but rather closely collaborates with the Ministry of Finance and other government administrative agencies—so much so that the president of the Bank of Japan and the Minister of Finance are usually jointly praised or blamed for favorable or unfavorable business (especially financial) conditions. Moreover, the Bank of Japan, while sharing with the Federal Reserve System the ability to restrain effective demand (to prevent inflation), nevertheless seems more interested in stimulating demand and particularly investment demand (toward the goal of cyclical recovery and secular growth). The basic reason for this effectiveness on the part of the Bank of Japan lies in the crucial dependence of Japanese business on commercial bank credit, which in turn depends largely on the lending policy of the central bank. On the other hand, any "cheap money" policy that the Federal Reserve System may adopt to stimulate demand is often frustrated by the conflicting policies of non-member banks and independent financial institutions, by the dependence of American business on internal financing and the capital market for expansion, and more recently by persistent balance of payments difficulties requiring a "dear money" policy to minimize gold outflows.[21]

Large metropolitan banks are the chief direct suppliers of investible funds in Japan. As mentioned earlier, these banks (which do the most shareholding) have an interlocking financial relationship with large business firms (which do the most investing), a rather peculiar relationship which accounts not only for the strategic role of long-term bank credit in postwar Japan's rapid growth[22] but also for the relative backwardness of its capital market and particularly of its flotation market.[23] It is interesting, by contrast, that their American counterparts specialize in short-term credit extensions to business firms or consumers (for the purchase of cars and home improvements), though longer-term loans are beginning to be extended to business.[24] The Japan Development Bank,[25] the Export-Import Bank, the Agriculture, Forestry, and Fishery Finance Corporation, the Housing Finance Corporation, and other governmental banks are instrumental in supplementing the commercial banks'

[21] See various issues of the Federal Reserve *Bulletin*, the *Federal Reserve Bank of New York Monthly Review*, and the President's Economic Report.

[22] Eguchi, "Keizai Seicho To Tsuika Shinyo."

[23] During the ten-year period 1955 to 1965 only 20 percent of total capital funds was raised annually in the regular capital market (see Y. Yamamoto, "Business Profits and Capital Structure," in *Japan Economic Research Center Monthly Report*, September 1965).

[24] Cf. G. Budzeika, "Commercial Banks as Suppliers of Capital Funds to Business," *Federal Reserve Bank of New York Monthly Review*, December 1963.

[25] It is interesting to note parenthetically that Dr. Shimomura, the famous initiator of postwar Japan's growth controversy and the intellectual father of former Prime Minister Ikeda's Income-Doubling Plan, happens to be an executive director of the Japan Development Bank. I am impressed by the additional fact that Mr. Eguchi, whose article is cited above, was originally on the staff of the Japan Development Bank.

supplies of capital funds, albeit on a more selective basis. The lending policies of these governmental banks generally transcend the usual commercial criteria of self-liquidation, profit maximization, and credit risks in accordance with the broader national priorities predetermined by public policy; their capital stocks are solely or partly subscribed by the government (to the latter quasi-governmental banks securing capital in part from the private sector belong the Central Cooperative Bank of Agriculture and Forestry and the Central Bank for Commercial and Industrial Cooperatives). The financial institutions at the bottom of the hierarchy are helpful to small business and consumers, but their contribution to the total supply of capital funds is insignificant.

Postwar Japan's heavy dependence on all sorts of credit for rapid economic growth is further indicated in Tables 21 and 22. The drastic reversal of the structure of capital funds from the prewar to the postwar period seen in Table 21 reflects the postwar need for investible funds far in excess of

Table 21.   *The Structure of Capital Funds*

Period	Borrowed Capital*	Owned Capital**
1934-36	40%(–)	60%(+)
1950-64	70%(+)	30%(–)

SOURCE: adapted from Y. Yamamoto, "Business Profits and Capital Structure," in *Japan Economic Research Center Monthly Report*, September 1965; Y. Uchiki et al., "The Consciousness and Behavior of Top-Management," *ibid.*
   *That part of total capital funds which is raised through bank loans, bond flotations, and interfirm borrowings.
   **Paid-in capital stock and corporate savings (including depreciation and other reserves).

ordinary business savings and corporate reserves. During the 1950–64 period corporations as a whole raised more than 70 percent of their total capital through borrowing, on the average. It is, therefore, not surprising that private investment during the ten-year period 1955 to 1965 depended on bank loans for 50 percent of its total financing, on retained profits (business savings including depreciation reserves) for 30 percent, and on new flotations in the capital market for 20 percent.[26] However, inasmuch as this last source of investible funds is "a variation of bank loans under the circumstances prevailing in Japan," as Professor Y. Hayashi has pointed out,[27] Japanese private investment actually seems to have relied upon bank credit for 70 percent of its total financing, at any rate during the postwar period. Professor Hayashi's comment refers to the Japanese practice whereby large banks buy up almost all the new shares floated and thus extend credit to corporations

[26] See Yamamoto, "Business Profits and Capital Structure."
[27] See Hayashi, "Capital Accumulation and Taxation in Japan."

Table 22.   Comparative Money-Capital Structures

Country	Borrowed Capital (external financing)	Owned Capital (internal financing)
U.S.	30%	70%
West Germany	40%	60%
Japan	70%	30%

SOURCE: adapted from Federation of Economic Organizations, *Japan Striving for Better Global Co-operation*, p. 11. The percentage figures are rough estimates for 1965.

trying to raise capital in the flotation market. This practice is facilitated by the exemption of capital reserves and intercorporate dividends from tax payments, for the corporations do not have to pay taxes on the capital reserves raised by selling their new shares to the banks, while the banks are completely exempt from taxes on the dividends accruing from their intercorporate shareholdings. This exemplifies both the inseparable relation of fiscal and monetary practices and the subtle relationship between large banks and big business in postwar Japan. [28]

Table 22 provides an international comparison of money-capital structures. "Borrowed capital" represents the external financing of potential investment, while "owned capital" represents the internal financing of it. We can see that Japanese business firms depend on external financing much more heavily than their American and German counterparts do, on the average. This great disparity between Japan's capital structure and those of the U.S. and West Germany may be explained in four ways: there are a larger number of business firms with insufficient net profits to plow back into investment in Japan than in the other two countries; there is heavier taxation of corporate income (vis-à-vis personal incomes) to reduce retained profits and capital reserves in Japan than in the other countries; there are more liberal (and irrational) corporate dividend payment policies in Japan (with less regard to cyclical changes in corporate earnings) than in the others; and the capital market is less well equipped to encourage external (and indirect) financing through bank loans in Japan than in the other countries. However, the disparity between Japan's money-capital structure and those of other advanced industrial countries is likely to become smaller and smaller as time goes on, judging from the Japanese Economic Planning Agency's 1965 White Paper, which strongly recommends the improvement of the money-capital structure (i.e., a higher ratio of owned capital and a lower ratio of borrowed capital to total capital funds) as fundamental to stable growth.

[28] Professor Hayashi makes this pertinent remark: "In fact the lifting of taxes on intercorporate dividends has expedited financial affiliation of banks to the industrial and business firms of their choice and further concentration of their loans in the firms so affiliated" (*ibid.*).

Since the Planning Agency does not specify the basis for its recommendation, we may suggest here several reasons[29] why Japanese economists and policymakers are concerned with the persistent "overloan" tendency in general and with what they call *shihonkosei akka* (the worsening structure of money capital) in particular: the sacrifice of independent investment decision-making by business firms which depend excessively on external financing for expansion; the undue predominance of finance capital (representing the large banks which do the most intercorporate shareholding and the most lending) over industrial capital (representing business firms which do the most investing); the excessively high proportion of capital charges in the total cost of production relative to total revenue, weakening firms' risk-taking ability as well as the country's competitive position in the world market; the danger that credit-supported investment in plant and equipment may lead to excess capacity, intensifying a recession; the danger that credit-induced investment demand may lead to the multiplier expansion of effective demand, aggravating a demand-pull inflation; and the exaggeration of cyclical instability because of the increasing effect of a low ratio of owned capital to total capital on dividend payments (and on implied spending) during a boom and its decreasing effect on net profits during a slump.

However, this list of the reasons for more or less micro and short-period concern with the "overloan" tendency cannot be accepted as an adequate explanation from a broader and longer view. Here we must turn to a more rigorous analysis of the role of credit in the secular growth of the Japanese economy. For this purpose I shall build, below, a simple model[30] to illustrate the effects of investment-geared credit on the demand and supply sides of the growing Japanese economy, with a view to indicating a technical condition of stable growth with full employment but without secular inflation. Such a model would, I believe, throw additional light on Japan's "overloan" controversy.

Postwar Japan's savings-investment equilibrium condition might be thought of as taking the special form

$$(3.1) \quad S + D = I_s + I_d$$

where S is savings, D is bank credit earmarked for private investment, I_s is savings-financed net investment, and I_d is credit-financed net investment. If savings-financed investment and credit-financed investment of (3.1) are increased, they will expand effective demand via the familiar multiplier mechanism:

[29] Some of these reasons are suggested by various critics of the Economic Planning Agency's White Paper in *Japan Economic Research Center Monthly Report*, September 1965.

[30] For alternative models, see Eguchi, "Keizai Seicho To Tsuika Shinyo," and the Appendix to this volume.

(3.2) $\Delta Y^d = k(\Delta I_s + \Delta I_d)$

where Y^d is the level of effective demand and k is the multiplier. Here an increment of credit-financed investment (ΔI_d) acts as a multiplicand on a par with an increment of savings-financed investment (ΔI_s), the multiplier being the reciprocal of the marginal propensities to save, to tax, and to import $[k = 1/(s + z + m)]$.

These increments of investment in equation (3.2) can be considered as definite fractions of effective demand for operational purposes:

(3.3) $\dfrac{\Delta I_s}{Y_d} = i, \ \dfrac{\Delta I_d}{Y_d} = d$

which ratios are both manipulative potential policy parameters from the standpoint of the fiscal-monetary authorities.

Taking (3.3) into account and dividing equation (3.2) through by Y_d yields

(3.4) $G^d \equiv \dfrac{\Delta Y^d}{Y_d} = k(i + d)$

which shows the possibility of the rate of growth of effective demand (G^d) increasing as a result of a higher ratio of additional credit-financed investment to effective demand $[\Delta d(t) > 0]$ when k and i remain constant $[\Delta k(t), \Delta i(t) = 0]$. Equation (3.4) represents the demand side of the credit-supported growing Japanese economy. It is this G^d which must be brought into equality with any given rate of growth of productive capacity if there is to be stable growth.

The absolute levels of savings-financed investment and credit-financed investment appearing in equation (3.1) are capable of expanding productive capacity via the production function of the form

(3.5) $\Delta Y^s = \sigma(\Delta K_s + \Delta K_d) = \sigma(I_s + I_d)$

where Y^s is the level of productive capacity, K_s is savings-financed capital input, K_d is credit-financed capital input, and σ is the productivity of capital (marginal = average assumed). Here the increments of the respective capital inputs are equivalent to savings-financed net investment and credit-financed net investment $(\Delta K_s \equiv I_s, \ \Delta K_d \equiv I_d)$.

The ratio of savings-financed investment to output is, in equilibrium, equal to the savings ratio (average). Likewise, the ratio of credit-financed investment to output is, in equilibrium, equal to the ratio of investment-earned credit to output. Accordingly, we can have

$$(3.6) \quad \frac{I_s}{Y^s} = \frac{S}{Y^s} \equiv s, \ \frac{I_d}{Y^s} = \frac{D}{Y^s} \equiv \delta$$

of which ratios δ is the more manipulative in nature.

Taking (3.6) into account and dividing equation (3.5) through by Y^s gives

$$(3.7) \quad G^s = \frac{\Delta Y^s}{Y^s} = \sigma(s + \delta),$$

which indicates the possibility of the rate of growth of productive capacity increasing as a consequence of a larger credit ratio $[\Delta\delta(t) > 0]$ when the savings ratio and capital productivity remain unchanged $[\Delta s(t), \Delta\sigma(t) = 0]$.

It follows that the Japanese economy would have to satisfy the following condition of equilibrium:

$$(3.8) \quad G^d = G^s \text{ or } k(i + d) - \sigma(s + \delta) = 0$$

which is the technical basis of stable growth with full employment but without secular inflation. Equation (3.8) carries with it these logical implications for a full-employment economy: if $k(i + d) - \sigma(s + \delta) > 0$, then there is secular inflation (due to excess demand); if $k(i + d) - \sigma(s + \delta) < 0$, then there is secular deflation (due to excess capacity). The equilibrium condition specified by (3.8), moreover, suggests that the monetary authority should deliberately manipulate the trend value of d relative to those of i and k on the demand side as well as the trend value of δ relatively to those of s and σ on the supply side if the Japanese economy is to maintain its stable growth of output with full employment and without inflation or deflation.

CHAPTER EIGHT

TECHNOLOGICAL PROGRESS AND PRODUCTIVITY GAINS

So conscious are the Japanese as a nation of their inherent paucity of resources and so determined are they to overcome it through technology that *gōrika* ("rationalization") and *kindaika* ("modernization") are household words in postwar Japan. There is a general tendency to regard technology as the *deus ex machina* to be called upon for solving all the growing pains of the Japanese economy. It is therefore no wonder that Schumpeter's insistence upon "innovation" made a smashing hit with Japanese economists and policy-makers,[1] especially in postwar conditions.

This chapter will deal with the role of technology in the growing Japanese economy; specifically, I shall discuss in this chapter the diverse effects of technological changes on labor productivity, labor cost, employment, capital intensity, the capital-output ratio, and overall growth rates of productive capacity. I shall also comment on the "technological controversy" among Japanese economists and policymakers and indicate wherein I differ from Japanese Schumpeterian theorists and practitioners.

By way of introduction, let me list the causes and effects of postwar Japan's single-minded quest for more and better know-how in the economic field. It is necessary to bear in mind the possibility of today's cause becoming tomorrow's effect, which effect may itself become a cause the day after tomorrow, and so on *ad infinitum* in so dynamic an economy as the Japanese. Abstracting from such cyclical interdependence, we may look first at a "still picture" of *causes*, namely, the general stimulation of international postwar nuclear and space developments and freer exchanges of technical inventions and innovations among nations; the loss of colonial sources of raw materials, intensifying Japan's inherent scarcity of natural resources; the urgency of keeping up with the international Joneses occasioned by the wide gap

---

[1] Exemplified by the Japan Management Association's 1960 *Gijitsu To Nihon Keizai* [Technology and the Japanese economy] jointly prepared by the research economists of its Productivity Research Institute (N. Oda, Y. Masuda, S. Yamazaki, and T. Nomura). See also Science and Technology Agency (a government agency within the Office of the Prime Minister), *White Paper on Science and Technology* (Tokyo, 1962).

between the defeated Japan's technological level and that of other industrial countries; the compelling need to improve the quality of capital so as to supplement its scarcity relative to expanding output; the gradual disappearance of labor reserves in the rural area of the country, the preponderant expansion of labor-intensive service industries, and the upward pressure of fully employed, newly liberated organized labor on money wages—all prompting the automation drive by cost-conscious producers; and the paternalistic and nationalistic state policy of encouraging (via selective subsidies, tax remissions, etc.) those industries which are considered most likely to do the innovating necessary for rapid growth relative to other advanced industrial economies.

Some of these causal factors will be amplified in due course. Meanwhile, let us turn to the following catalogue of effects: the opening up of new investment opportunities and the accompanying expansion of "innovational investment" relative to effective demand or productive capacity; the downward pressure of import-substituting industrialization on the import ratio, coupled with the upward pressure of cost-reducing methods of production on the export ratio; a decreasing impact on the capital-output ratio, coupled with an increasing impact on labor productivity, especially in manufacturing industries; a structural shift to highly technologized heavy industries (especially machine, electronic, chemical, and automotive); temporary technological unemployment, albeit without disrupting the continuous state of full employment; and an increase in the "gadget-consciousness" of the consuming public and a rapid shift to consumer durables (especially television sets, washing machines, electric refrigerators, and automobiles).

Some of these effects will be amplified in subsequent discussions, but the above catalogue, together with that of causes, seems sufficient to indicate the nature and direction of technological progress in the growing Japanese economy. With this as our general background, we may proceed to specify some empirical findings on postwar Japan's technological changes and impacts.

TECHNOLOGY, LABOR PRODUCTIVITY, AND EMPLOYMENT

Perhaps the most spectacular effect of technological progress in postwar Japan can be seen in the rapidly rising productivity of labor and the consequent falling efficiency labor cost[2] of its manufacturing industries as a whole, as shown in Table 23. We must be careful not to draw rash inferences from the data in the table, for the following reasons. It concerns the productive performance of the manufacturing sector alone, however strategic that sector may be in and by itself. The relatively less productive agricultural and

---

[2] Let real wages = W, employment = N, and labor productivity = Y/N. Then we can have efficiency labor cost = $(W/N)/(Y/N)$ for any sector in any period.

Table 23. *Labor Productivity and Efficiency Labor Cost in Manufacturing Industries, 1952-61*

Year	Labor Productivity*	Efficiency Labor Cost*
1952	77	104
1955	100	100
1958	115	82
1961	159	45

SOURCE: the figures for labor productivity are from the Ministry of Labor's 1961 *Yearbook of Labor Statistics* and are in real terms (i.e., in 1955 constant prices). The figures for efficiency labor cost were calculated by the author on the basis of the indices of real wages, employment, and labor productivity provided in the same yearbook for the periods involved. The computational method is indicated in footnote 2 to this chapter.

*Base year, 1955.

service sectors considerably offset the productivity gains of the manufacturing sector, with the net result that labor productivity and efficiency labor cost for the whole economy would be much smaller and much higher, respectively, than is shown in the table. (Recall the sectoral comparisons in Chapter 6.) The falling efficiency labor cost, while helpful to the exportation of labor-intensive manufactures (as in Japan's trade vis-à-vis low-income countries), nevertheless would not be so helpful to the exportation of capital-intensive manufactures, whose labor cost is a smaller proportion of total cost (as in Japan's trade vis-à-vis high-income countries). Last, movements of organized labor toward higher wages in conditions of full employment, coupled with the seniority wage system mentioned earlier, might conceivably increase money wages (W_m) relative to the given price index (p) and so increase the real wage rate $[W/N = (W_m/p)/N]$ much faster than labor productivity (Y/N) in the future. Then the ratio measuring efficiency labor cost $[= (W/N)/(Y/N)]$ could rise, contrary to the trend shown in Table 23. This constitutes a warning against any complacent view of the Japanese economy's competitive position in the world market, as well as of its productive efficiency at home, that overenthusiastic Schumpeterians might entertain.

The above reservations seem to be indirectly justified by the Japanese Economic Planning Agency's cautious extrapolation of Japan's overall labor productivity trend, as shown in Table 24. The table indicates the seemingly paradoxical downward trend of labor productivity for the whole Japanese economy despite the upward trend of general technology. The Economic Planning Agency provides no answer to this paradox. One possible answer is that there are many determinants of labor productivity other than technological progress, especially in the Japanese economy with its traditional permanent employment practice and the seniority wage payment system

Table 24.   The Growth Rate of Labor Productivity

Period	Average Annual Growth Rate
1950-60	7.0% (realized)
1960-70	6.1% (projected)

SOURCE: adapted from CED, *Japan in the Free World Economy*, p. 56. The percentage figure for the 1950-60 period is based on data from Bureau of Statistics, Office of the Prime Minister, while that for 1960-70 is based on the Economic Planning Agency's *New Long-Range Economic Plan of Japan*.

obstructing the mobility of labor from less productive to more productive industries or sectors. That the average annual growth rate of labor productivity is not expected to fall very significantly in the 1960s partly reflects the offsetting effects of such non-technological factors as the effect of the rising general level of education and the increasing scale of welfare statecraft upon the intelligence, vigor, and motivation of the working population. Nevertheless, the relevant point to be made about the table is that the rate of technological progress in the economic field is expected to decline at an equal rate with domestic industrialization relative to foreign industrialization, slowing down the rate of growth of labor productivity in the decades ahead. We shall return to this point later when we come to the "technological controversy." Meanwhile, the comparative productivity data in Table 25 are of interest.

Table 25 strongly intimates the cause-and-effect interdependence of the four top-growth countries (Japan, Italy, France, and West Germany) as far as manufacturing industries are concerned. Rapid overall growth induces greater

Table 25.   International Labor Productivities in Manufacturing Industries* (1950-60 averages)

Country	Growth Rate of Manufacturing Labor Productivity
	%
Japan	12.2
Italy	7.6
France	5.8
West Germany	5.1
U.S.	2.7
U.K.	2.3
Denmark	2.1

*Adapted from Kamakura, *Nihon Keizairon*, p. 35, based on UN, *Statistical Yearbook*, and OECD, *General Statistical Bulletin*.

"innovational investment" in the manufacturing sector and is in turn induced by that investment. The low rates of growth of labor productivity in the American, British, and Danish manufacturing industries are not to be taken as prima facie evidence of their overall rates of growth of labor productivity. The American economy, for instance, achieved an overall 3.2 percent trend rate of growth of labor productivity during the fairly comparable 1947–65 period,[3] even though its manufacturing sector's counterpart was 2.7 percent during the 1950–60 period. This suggests the possibility that the labor productivities of the agricultural and service sectors in the American, British, and Danish economies grew fast enough to compensate for the relatively low rates of growth of labor productivity in their manufacturing sectors.

Conversely, the superlative 12.2 percent rate of growth of labor productivity of the manufacturing sector for the 1950–60 period must have been considerably offset by the relatively slow growth of labor productivity in the agricultural and service sectors.[4] Table 24 showed that the Japanese economy as a whole experienced a much lower rate of growth of labor productivity during the same period. Nevertheless, the main point here is that if Japan's manufacturing industries had not achieved a 12.2 percent rate of growth of labor productivity, the rate of growth of labor productivity for the whole economy could not have been as high as 7 percent, a figure that is more than twice that of the U.S. (3.2 percent).

It is interesting, in this connection, to observe that, whereas the American economy is greatly concerned with the persistence of technological unemployment because of spreading automation,[5] the rapidly growing Japanese economy is more interested in the favorable repercussion of automation upon its labor productivity. Thus the authors of *Technology and the Japanese Economy*, for example, were able to dispel the common fear of technological unemployment effectively by calling attention to the full growth of full employment in Japan not in spite of, but because of, automation and other productivity-increasing innovations.[6] Likewise, Dr. O. Shimomura argues that "a rapidly growing economy, while including employment-decreasing technological progress, nevertheless expands high-quality employment opportunities fairly rapidly and so actually strengthens its basic ability to utilize more and cheaper products."[7] I am reminded of Keynes's optimistic view of

[3] National Commission on Technology, Automation, and Economic Progress (H. R. Bowen, Chairman), *Technology and the American Economy* (Washington, D.C., 1966), vol. 1, p. 15.

[4] Fairly steady declines in the labor productivities of the agricultural and service sectors occurred from 1947 to 1955, according to Professor K. Ohkawa (see his *The Growth Rate of the Japanese Economy since 1878*, p. 240). I have not seen any later data that would contradict my a priori view of slowly growing labor productivities in those non-manufacturing sectors after 1955.

[5] National Commission on Technology, Automation, and Economic Progress, *Technology and the American Economy*, vol. 1.

[6] Japan Management Association, *Gijitsu To Nihon Keizai.*

[7] See I. Nakayama, ed., *Nihon Keizai No Seicho*, p. 122.

technological unemployment as "a temporary phase of maladjustment" and his assurance that "all this means in the long run *that mankind is solving its economic problem.*"[8] Neither Keynes nor Shimomura has provided a technical demonstration to justify his assertion. We might digress here to discuss technical conditions to be satisfied for continuous full employment in an *automating* economy.[9]

To sharpen the issue, let us begin with the employment function of a non-automating economy,

$$(1.1) \quad N_t = \bar{n} Y_t \quad (n \equiv N/Y = \text{const.})$$

where N_t is the amount of labor demanded or simply employment, Y is full-capacity output, and $\bar{n}$ is the constant labor-output ratio in the given state of technology. Equation (1.1) implies

$$(1.2) \quad \Delta N_t = \bar{n} \Delta Y_t$$

From (1.1) and (1.2) we get

$$(1.3) \quad \left(\frac{\Delta N}{N}\right)_t = \frac{\bar{n} \Delta Y_t}{\bar{n} Y_t} = \left(\frac{\Delta Y}{Y}\right)_t = \frac{s}{b} \quad (\textit{non}\text{-automating case})$$

where $\Delta N/N$ is the rate of growth of employment, $\Delta Y/Y$ is the rate of growth of full-capacity output, s is the constant savings ratio, and b is the constant capital-output ratio. Equation (1.3) tells us that the rate of growth of employment is the same as the rate of growth of full-capacity output when technological progress is neither labor-saving nor labor-using, so as to leave the labor-output ratio unaltered over time. It implies that capital and output must grow at a rate determined by the technical relation of the savings ratio and the capital-output ratio (in the Harrod-Domar formulation) in order to maintain continuous full employment.

Now introduce automation in the form of labor-saving devices of all sorts. Every invention and innovation tending to reduce the amount of labor required per unit of output gives rise to a downward movement in the labor-output ratio $[\Delta n(t) < 0]$. Then we have a new dynamic employment function of the form

$$(1.4) \quad N_t = n_t Y_t \quad (n \neq \text{const.}, \ t = 0, \ 1)$$

---

[8] See Keynes, *Essays in Persuasion*, p. 364.

[9] For further details, see my *The Keynesian Theory of Economic Development* (New York, 1959) (esp. chaps. 5 and 6).

of which Y and n are specifiable as

(1.5) $Y_t = Y_0(1 + g)^t$ $(g \equiv \Delta Y/Y = s/b)$

(1.6) $n_t = n_0/(1 + v)^t$ $(v \equiv \Delta n/n)$

Here Y_0 and n_0 are, respectively, the initial values of the variables g, the rate of growth (average annual) of full-capacity output, and v, the rate of decrease in the labor-output ratio (due to automation).

Let employment grow according to

(1.7) $N_t = N_0(1 + \epsilon)^t$ $(\epsilon \equiv \Delta N/N)$

where ϵ is the rate of growth of employment in an automating economy to be determined by reference to equations (1.4)–(1.6) and implicit equation $N_0 = n_0 Y_0$ for the initial period:

$$(1.8) \quad \epsilon = \frac{N_t}{N_0} - 1 = \frac{\dfrac{n_0}{1 + \gamma} Y_0 \left(1 + \dfrac{s}{b}\right)}{n_0 Y_0} - 1$$

$$= \frac{1 + \dfrac{s}{b}}{1 + \gamma} - 1 \quad \text{(automating case)}$$

The rate of growth of employment given by (1.8) includes the decreasing impact of automation, and is obviously smaller than that given by (1.3) without automation. The amount of labor required in the automating economy expressed by (1.8) can grow only at a rate equal to

$$(1.9) \quad 1 + \epsilon = \frac{1 + \dfrac{s}{b}}{1 + v}$$

instead of a rate equal to $1 + (s/b)$.

Suppose that the labor force (N') grows according to

(1.10) $N_t' = N_0'(1 + \lambda)^t$ $(\lambda \equiv \Delta N'/N', \ t = 1, 0)$

where λ is the demographically and culturally given rate of growth of the labor force. From (1.9) and (1.10) we can derive an expression measuring persistent technological unemployment:

$$(1.11) \quad \frac{1 + \frac{s}{b}}{1 + \nu} - (1 + \lambda) < 0$$

although the actual existence of such technological unemployment would have to be proved by reference to the behavior of the labor force (N'_t) relative to that of technologically reduced employment (N_t).

It follows that the full employment equilibrium condition to be satisfied by our automating growing economy is given by

$$(1.12) \quad \frac{1 + \frac{s}{b}}{1 + \nu} = 1 + \lambda; \; 1 + \frac{s}{b} = (1 + \nu)(1 + \lambda)$$

which implies that capital and output in such an economy must expand at a rate equal to

$$(1.13) \quad \frac{s}{b} = (1 + \pi)(1 + \lambda) - 1 \quad (\pi \equiv \Delta\rho/\rho)$$
$$= \pi + \lambda \text{ for } \lambda\pi \sim 0$$

[see equations (2.1)–(2.6) also] if persistent technological unemployment is to be wiped out completely.

Turning now to the more positive side of technology, we may now ponder the implications for the growth of productive capacity of an increasing labor productivity due to technological progress. For the labor-scarce kind of economy discussed in Chapter 6, which seems to be the common lot of all affluent societies including Japan, it is a matter of crucial importance to adopt such inventions and innovations (along with high educational standards) in order to continue increasing the rate of growth of labor productivity. Sir Roy Harrod's concept of the "natural" rate of growth[10] will come of age in a way that Schumpeter or the Keynes of *Essays in Persuasion*[11] (rather than of the *General Theory*) might not have fully anticipated.

Recall that the Japanese Economic Planning Agency estimated the trend rate of growth of labor productivity for the 1960-70 period to be 6.1 per-

[10] See R. F. Harrod, *Towards a Dynamic Economics* (London, 1948).

[11] Keynes, while taking the state of technology as given in his short-run theory of employment (1936), nevertheless made this long-run observation earlier (1930): "From the sixteenth century, with a cumulative crescendo after the eighteenth, the great age of science and technical inventions began, which has been in full flood—coal, steam, electricity, petrol, steel, rubber, cotton, the chemical industries, automatic machinery and the methods of mass production, wireless, printing, Newton, Darwin, and Einstein, and thousands of other things and men too famous and familiar to catalogue" (see his "Economic Possibilities for Our Grandchildren," in *Essays in Persuasion*, p. 363).

cent, according to Table 24. It also estimated the rate of growth of the labor force for the same period to be 1.0 percent.[12] It is, then, hardly surprising that the agency should have projected 7.1 percent as the feasible rate of growth of productive capacity (real GNP) over the 1960–70 horizon,[13] for we know that the rate of growth of productive capacity in a capital-abundant yet labor-scarce economy equals the rate of growth of labor productivity plus the rate of growth of the labor force.[14] Applying the above numerical values, we get for the Japanese economy[15] $g = 0.061 + 0.01 = 0.071$, or 7.1 percent. We arrive at this rate of growth of productive capacity as follows:

$$(2.1) \quad Y_0 = \rho_0 N_0 \quad (\rho \equiv Y/N)$$

$$(2.2) \quad Y_t = \rho_t N_t \quad (t = 0, 1)$$

$$(2.3) \quad N_t = N_0(1 + \lambda)^t \quad (\lambda \equiv \Delta N/N)$$

$$(2.4) \quad \rho_t = \rho_0(1 + \pi)^t \quad (\pi \equiv \Delta\rho/\rho)$$

$$(2.5) \quad Y_t = Y_0(1 + g)^t \quad (g \equiv \Delta Y/Y)$$

$$(2.6) \quad g = \frac{\Delta Y_t}{Y_0} - 1 = \frac{\rho_0(1 + \pi)N_0(1 + \lambda)}{\rho_0 N_0} - 1$$

$$= (1 + \pi)(1 + \lambda) - 1$$

$$= \lambda + \pi \text{ for } \pi\lambda \sim 0$$

Here Y is output, N is full employment labor (the labor force when fully employed), ρ is the average productivity of labor determined by technological change, λ is the rate of growth of the fully employed labor force predetermined by population growth and capital accumulation, in a manner indicated by equation (1.13), π is the rate of growth of labor productivity predetermined by automation and education, g is the average annual rate of growth of productive capacity, and t is time.

[12] Japanese Economic Planning Agency, *New Long-Range Economic Plan of Japan, 1961–1970* (Tokyo, 1961).

[13] *Ibid.*

[14] See my *The Keynesian Theory of Economic Development*, p. 45, n. 1; also my *National Income and Economic Growth* (Chicago, 1961), p. 154. The versions given in these two books are rather less rigorous than the version given in the text above.

[15] It is interesting that Governor Nelson A. Rockefeller used the same method of estimating g for the American economy: "Over the post-war period, U.S. productivity as measured by output per man-hour increased by 3% a year. The work force increase averaged 1.4% a year. That should have given a GNP growth rate of 4.4%. But it did not. Work hours on average declined 0.6% each year, so that our GNP increase averaged only 3.8%" (see *Accelerated Economic Growth*, p. 15). In other words, for the American economy we had $g = 0.03 + (0.014 - 0.006) = 0.038$ or 3.8 percent, according to Governor Rockefeller.

Equation (2.1) gives a special production function in the initial period based on the structural assumptions that labor is the limiting factor of production and that capital cannot be bodily substituted for labor in the preponderantly labor-intensive process of production (as in an advanced economy with the disproportionately rapid expansion of the tertiary sector discussed in Chapter 6). Equations (2.2)-(2.5) are self-explanatory in view of the definitions of the variables involved. Equation (2.6) is derived from equations (2.1)-(2.5) and tells us that the rate of growth of productive capacity (g) amounts to the sum of the rate of growth of the fully employed labor force (λ) and the rate of growth of technologically influenced labor productivity (π). It indicates the theoretical possibility that output grows faster with a large π when λ remains constant. It is interesting, in connection with equation (2.6), to note that the Japanese economy relies primarily on a higher rate of growth of labor productivity (a large π) according to its Economic Planning Agency,[16] whereas the American economy counts principally on a higher rate of growth of the labor force (a larger λ) according to Governor Rockefeller.[17] Thus it appears that the Japanese economy is rather more Schumpeterian in orientation than the American economy.

TECHNOLOGY AND THE CAPITAL-OUTPUT RATIO

The nature and direction of technological progress are capable of influencing the long-run behavior of the capital-output ratio, which is one of the strategic determinants of economic growth. Indeed, a large part of postwar Japan's growth controversy has been centered upon the concept, measurement, and stability of the capital coefficient or its reciprocal, capital productivity.[18] Dr. O. Shimomura went as far as to predict a 10 percent rate of growth for the Japanese economy over the 1961-70 planning horizon (the Income-Doubling Plan of the Ikeda administration) partly on the debatable assumption that capital productivity will continue to be as high as 1 or 100 percent. This implies, according to Shimomura's growth model of the Harrod-Domar type, that the Japanese economy could maintain a 10 percent rate of growth by saving 10 percent of its national income annually, for if

[16] *Ibid.*

[17] *Ibid.* (presumably through fairer employment practices, less work stoppages, more gradual reductions in working hours, better management-labor relations, etc.).

[18] For conceptual and statistical debates on the capital coefficient, see O. Shimomura, "Seicho Seisaku No Kihon Mondai" [Basic problems of growth policy], *Nihon Keizeigaku*, March, 1961; and various polemical comments by Professors Y. Shionoya, K. Baba, and M. Shinohara, in *ibid.* See also Nakayama, ed., *Nihon Keizai No Seicho*, and Ichimura, *Sekai No Nakano Nihon Keizai*, p. 157ff. All these commentators are largely concerned with what should go into the denominator of the ratio $\Delta Y/I$ or whether the numerator should be in gross or net terms rather than with exploring fundamental determinants of the behavior of that ratio. For a discussion of such determinants, see my "Technological Flexibility and 'Golden Age' Equilibrium Growth," *Indian Economic Journal*, January-March 1967.

capital productivity (σ) = 1.00 and the savings ratio (s) = 0.10, then the growth rate (g) = 1.00 $\times$ 0.10 = 0.10 or 10 percent (since g = σs). Apart from the controversial question of how Dr. Shimomura arrives at such a high capital productivity figure, it is obvious that he presumes a highly efficient allocation of capital resources or a high quality of capital, or both, for the postwar Japanese economy. The only light that his concept of capital productivity throws on the possible connection between technology and the capital coefficient comes from his deliberate and exclusive choice of private fixed investment in plant and equipment, which is most closely associated with postwar Japan's modernization-rationalization drive. His choice is based on the debatable grounds that private fixed investment is not only high but stable over the long run and that public investment is generally unproductive (as though postwar Japan's public investment included the pyramid-building type of military investment and other obviously wasteful, non-capacity-increasing projects).

Some economists on the other side of the Pacific have been impressed by Japan's exceptionally low capital coefficient relative to that of the U.S. and other industrially advanced countries. Professor S. Kuznets reports that "the levels of the capital-output ratios for Japan were distinctly lower than in other countries . . . because the sectoral distribution and the capital-output ratios within sectors must have made for the possibility of large gains in output with relatively small inputs of additional capital."[19] Professor M. Bronfenbrenner makes the observation that "the main difference between the Japanese and American results for recent years lies in the higher capital productivity (now called more frequently the *lower* 'capital coefficient') in Japan."[20] Professor Bronfenbrenner attributes to Japan's high capital productivity such factors as "the higher Japanese ratio of labor to capital" (in contrast with "the American practice of rapid depreciation and obsolescence, and the higher degree of excess capacity in America") and "concentration on output-increasing investment in Japan" (that is, "as against cost-reducing investment in America").[21] Professor H. Rosovsky explains Japan's low capital coefficient by reference to "a mixed style of industrialization" which relies "both on labour-intensive indigenous and capital-intensive modern techniques."[22]

Let me now enumerate the structural determinants of the capital coefficient for all growing economies, with a view to singling out those which are particularly relevant to the modernizing and rationalizing Japanese economy:

[19]"Quantitative Aspects of the Economic Growth of Nations," *Economic Development and Cultural Change*, July, 1961.
[20]"Economic Miracles and Japan's Income-Doubling Plan."
[21]*Ibid.*
[22]"Capital Formation in Pre-War Japan: Current Findings and Future Problems."

(1) the stage of industrialization, with earlier stages requiring more capital-intensive bases of heavy industry (harbors, railroads, highways, airports, dams, etc.) and later stages requiring more labor-intensive services of all kinds;

(2) the nature and direction of technological progress affecting both labor productivity at the given level of capital intensity and the degree of capital intensity at the given level of labor productivity;

(3) the elasticity of substitution of capital for labor with respect to their relative factor prices in the given state of technology;

(4) the structure of investment-consumption demand, with the larger proportion of housing investment in total investment demand increasing capital relative to output and that of durables in total consumption demand entailing larger capital inputs;

(5) the existence of excess capacity regarded as a normal phenomenon in a cycle-sensitive or monopoly-ridden economy, obviating the necessity of increasing new investment to meet expanding demand;

(6) the relative abundance of capital and labor, leading to greater or smaller capital intensity at given levels of factor prices;

(7) the rate of depreciation and obsolescence as influenced by either physical wear and tear or competitive market pressure, increasing or decreasing replacement investment per unit of output;

(8) the quality of replacement capital at the given level of capital charges, with superior equipment replacing inferior equipment at the same cost but for greater output gains per unit of capital; and

(9) the nature and proportion of public investment, with the pyramid-building variety (especially military investment) tending to decrease output gains per unit of capital and the welfare-promoting variety (especially educational investment) tending to increase them.

I would argue that, of the structural determinants listed above, (1), (2), (4), (8), and (9) are particularly relevant to the postwar Japanese economy, and that all these determinants except (4) tend to decrease its capital coefficient over the long run. I have already indicated in earlier chapters the reasons why the Japanese economy is rapidly moving in the direction of a labor-intensive, service- (or tertiary-) dominated phase, a welfare-oriented public investment program, a labor-dependent production function, and a systematic fiscal-monetary aid scheme to encourage "modernization" and "rationalization" in selective industries, a direction which would require less and less capital per unit of output as well as per unit of labor. In this regard, I take exception to the widely held view of Japanese economists that the future expansion of public overhead capital formation would raise the level of the capital coefficient or lower the level of capital productivity, for I believe that the increasing demand for educational investment, fixed public investment in non-military equipment, and long-range welfare projects would entail, in the long run, larger and larger gains in output with the same inputs of capital or labor. Japanese economists are so accustomed to thinking of public investment in terms of traditional (prewar) outlays for the construction of battleships, fighter planes, and other armaments of a non-capacity-increasing nature that they seem to overlook the productivity-increasing aspects of the new Japan's public investment.

This oversight is coupled with academic economists' generally pessimistic view of the future of technology in the Japanese economy and with the corollary view that Japan's capital coefficient will show an upward trend after the present drive to catch up technologically is over. In connection with the cyclically rising marginal fixed capital-output ratio in the postwar Japanese economy (1946-59), Professor M. Shinohara observes: "The technological progress in recent years can be said to have narrowed the gap considerably, and if this gap is further narrowed in the future, then one might presume that the rate of Japan's economic growth would be slowed down."[23] He thereby implies that the cyclically rising capital coefficient might turn into a secularly rising one in the absence of such capital-saving, output-increasing innovations as would persist in the future were it not for the narrowing gap between Japan's technological level and those of more advanced economies. Similar views have been expressed by Professors K. Ara,[24] S. Ichimura,[25] and N. Kamakura.[26] All these rather pessimistic views ignore both Japan's inherent resource scarcity as a permanent stimulus for technological progress and the greater know-how of more advanced economies as a continuing challenge to Japan's technological efforts. Moreover, the pessimistic views of these academic economists must be balanced against the more optimistic view of such non-academics as Dr. O. Shimomura, who has called attention to the persistent gap between technologically advanced and technologically backward industries within the Japanese economy and to the implicit continuing scope for technological improvements.[27] I differ with Dr. Shimomura in

---

[23] Shinohara, *Growth and Cycles in the Japanese Economy*, pp. 13-14.

[24] See Ara's technological remark in Nakayama, ed., *Nihon Keizai No Seicho*, p. 102.

[25] See Ichimura's observations on the prospect of a falling off in technological progress as a result of Japan's drive to catch up and of a rising level of the capital coefficient accompanying a shift to presumably less productive public investment (*Sekai No Nakano Nihon Keizai*, pp. 148, 162).

[26] *Nihon Keizairon*, pp. 14-15.

[27] See Shimomura's argument in Nakayama, ed., *Nihon Keizai No Seicho*, pp. 13-14. Dr. Shimomura, moreover, seems to have implicit faith in the ability of labor to move freely from. agriculture and small-scale industries to more efficient large-scale industries based on modern technology. This faith is shared by Professor Kamakura (*Nihon Keizairon*, pp. 32-33). However, Professor Shinohara responds skeptically to Dr. Shimomura's optimism by pointing out a quantitatively significant shift of employment to the generally less efficient tertiary sector (see Nakayama, ed., *Nihon Keizai No Seicho*, p. 120).

thinking that capital productivity under the impetus of expanding "modern-ization" and "rationalization" would show an upward but not stable trend in the future Japanese economy.

The list of structural determinants given earlier is useful not only in testing hypotheses about the secular Japanese behavior of the capital-output ratio but also in interpreting such international data as are shown in Table 26. The table reveals that the top-growth countries of Japan, Italy, France, and Germany had relatively low capital coefficients during the 1958–62 period as well as during the 1950–58 period. It also confirms the observation of Professor Kuznets concerning the Japanese capital coefficient vis-à-vis other countries. In terms of 1958–62 levels, Japan's capital coefficient is lower than in any other country, implying the highest productivity of capital regarded as the reciprocal of the lowest capital-output ratio. In terms of 1950–62 trends, the capital coefficients of Japan, Italy, and the U.S. show a downward trend, while those of France, Germany, the U.S.S.R., and the U.K. show an upward trend. It is particularly interesting that Professor Ichimura, on whose data Table 26 is based, attributes the rising trend of the Soviet capital coefficient largely to a shortage of labor, which has made the U.S.S.R. rely more and more on capital accumulation for greater labor productivity, and partly to the increasing pressure of relatively unproductive public investment (presumably including military investment). [28]

Table 26. International Capital Coefficients

Country	1950–58	1958–62
Japan	1.5	0.9
Italy	3.8	2.7
France	3.4	3.6
West Germany	3.2	3.8
U.S.	6.3	5.3
U.S.S.R.	3.3	6.2
U.K.	5.9	6.4

SOURCE: adapted from Ichimura, *The Japanese Economy in the World*, p. 99. Each figure refers to the marginal capital-output ratio and has been derived from non-housing net investment divided by additional per capita output, according to Professor Ichimura.

I myself am inclined to believe that the trend values of capital coefficients in countries with labor shortage but without patently wasteful public invest-ment projects would be relatively small, especially if such countries tried to

[28] Ichimura, *Sekai No Nakano Nihon Keizai*, pp. 98–99.

meet labor shortages by increasing labor productivity through a combination of technological progress and educational investment. In view of the multiplicity of influences mentioned above, the extent to which technological progress by itself is instrumental in lowering the capital-output ratios of the top-growth countries in Table 26 remains conjectural. Still, it does seem plausible to presume that the relatively low capital coefficient of the Japanese economy owes a great deal to its technological drive, powerfully motivated by resource, capital, and, more recently, labor scarcity, to increase the productivities of capital and labor for rapid overall growth.

It might be convenient, at this juncture, to indicate the general effects of technological progress on the dynamic behavior of the capital-output ratio and hence on the rate of growth of productive capacity in an operationally significant way, as follows:

$$(3.1) \quad b \equiv \frac{K}{Y} = \frac{K}{N}\frac{N}{Y} = \frac{K/N}{Y/N} \equiv \frac{\theta}{\rho} \quad \left(b \equiv \frac{K}{Y} = \frac{\Delta K}{\Delta Y} \equiv \frac{I}{\Delta Y} \right)$$

$$(3.2) \quad \Delta\theta(t) < 0, \; \Delta\rho(t) = 0$$

$$(3.3) \quad \Delta b(t) < 0 \text{ for } \Delta\theta(t) < 0 \qquad \text{(independent case of less capital-intensive know-how; transistorization)}$$

$$(3.4) \quad \Delta\rho(t) > 0, \; \Delta\theta(t) = 0$$

$$(3.5) \quad \Delta b(t) < 0, \text{ for } \Delta\rho(t) > 0 \qquad \text{(independent case of labor-saving devices; automation)}$$

$$(3.6) \quad \eta(t) = \frac{\partial(\log \theta_t)}{\partial(\log \rho_t)} < 1$$

$$(3.7) \quad \Delta b(t) < 0, \text{ for } \eta(t) < 1 \qquad \text{(interdependent case of automation entailing less capital intensity)}$$

$$(3.8) \quad b(t) = \frac{b_0}{(1 + \zeta)^t}$$

$$(3.9) \quad s = s(t) = \bar{s}; \; \Delta s(t) = 0 \qquad (s \equiv S/Y)$$

$$(3.10) \quad g(t) \equiv \left(\frac{\Delta Y}{Y}\right)_t = \frac{s(t)}{b(t)} = \frac{\bar{s}}{b_0/(1 + \zeta)^t}$$

Here Y is national output, K is capital input (private and public), I is net investment, b is the capital-output ratio (marginal = average assumed), θ is the capital-labor ratio or capital intensity which measures the degree of "roundaboutness," ρ is the average productivity of labor, η is the trend value of the elasticity of capital intensity with respect to labor productivity, ζ is the rate of decrease in the capital coefficient, s is the average savings ratio, g is the rate of growth of productive capacity or output, and t is time.

Equation (3.1) shows that the capital-output ratio is a joint product of the capital-labor ratio and labor productivity, tending to vary directly with the former ratio and inversely with the latter. It is a formal counterpart of b among the structural determinants mentioned earlier and subsumes all other influences, on the plausible assumption that the nature and the direction of technological progress is the most representative and strategic independent variable influencing the secular behavior of the capital coefficient. Equation (3.2) expresses the specific assumption that the capital-labor ratio decreases because of such innovations as transistorization and miniaturization (widely adopted in postwar Japan), while labor productivity remains constant. It indicates one way in which technological progress can affect the capital-output ratio, that is, by requiring less capital per unit of labor in the productive process, quite independent of their factor prices. Equation (3.3) tells us that the dynamic capital coefficient decreases as a consequence of smaller capital intensity when labor productivity remains unchanged. Equation (3.4) expresses the assumption that labor productivity increases over time while capital intensity remains unaltered as a consequence of increasing output per unit of labor through widespread automation. (Here we are tacitly assuming that output expands fast enough to absorb temporarily displaced workers in a manner indicated in the first section of this chapter.) Equation (3.5) indicates that the dynamic capital coefficient can decrease as a result of an automation-induced higher labor productivity that is not accompanied by an offsetting change in capital intensity. Equation (3.6) expresses the assumption that the elasticity of capital intensity with respect to labor productivity is less than unity, on the plausible ground that an automation-facilitated increase in labor productivity leads to smaller capital inputs relative to labor inputs. Equation (3.7) shows the possibility of a decrease in the capital coefficient as a consequence of the interdependent effect specified by (3.6). Equation (3.8) tells us that the capital coefficient at time t decreases at the constant rate ζ, given the initial value of that coefficient b_0. It implies a rising trend of capital productivity. Equation (3.9) expresses the assumption that the savings ratio remains constant over time, a simplifying assumption made to isolate the technological role in overall growth. Finally, (3.10) gives us the rate of growth of output (Harrod-Domar), including the dynamic repercussions of technological progress on the capital coefficient specified by (3.3), (3.5), and (3.7).

Thus technological efforts to increase the productivity of capital ($1/b$), such as those associated with Japan's modernization-rationalization drive, are of special importance to the capital-scarce phase of economic development, in which the overwhelming majority of present-day developing economies find themselves. However, as those economies march on to the labor-scarce phase, technological efforts will have to be concentrated on increasing labor productivity in a manner indicated earlier in this chapter. The Japanese economy, driven by its few natural resources and its exposure to an age of nuclear-space technology, has no alternative but to exploit Schumpeterian innovation and explore Keynesian "possibilities for our grandchildren"—without, one hopes, putting all its eggs in one basket. [29]

[29] Even Schumpeter put a few eggs in the "entrepreneurship" and "credit" baskets, though the former must be broadened to embrace state initiative and risk-taking and the latter to include fiscally created subsidies and transfer payments, in the specific context of the Japanese economy.

CHAPTER NINE

ECONOMIC GROWTH WITHOUT SECULAR INFLATION

The Japanese economy is no exception to the universal quest for rapid growth without secular inflation, judging from the Economic Planning Agency's 1965 White Paper, which includes price stability as a national desideratum. The recent imbalance between the horizontal trend of wholesale prices and the upward trend of consumer prices has given rise to a heated controversy over an "income-doubling" plan vs. a "price-doubling" plot, "demand-pull" vs. "cost-push" inflation, and a "deflation-biased" vs. "inflation-biased" public policy. I shall discuss this controversy throughout this chapter. However, my principal purpose here is to analyze, empirically and theoretically, the structural forces determining the compatibility of economic growth and price stability in the postwar Japanese economy. This chapter will be divided into two sections, the first of which deals with the empirical background and the second with theoretical and practical considerations. The chapter as a whole may throw additional light on the relation of inflation and growth in general[1] and prospects of price stability for the growing Japanese economy in particular.[2]

[1] For divers general views on the subject, see G. S. Dorrance, "Inflation and Growth," *The Fund and Bank Review*, June 1964; F. Machlup, "The Finance of Development in Poor Countries: Foreign Capital and Domestic Inflation," *Riron Keizaigaku*, April 1956; and my "A Note on Inflation and Economic Development," *ibid.*, June 1957.

[2] For alternative interpretations of the Japanese situation, see Eguchi, "Keizai Seicho To Tsuika Shinyo"; R. S. Ozaki, "Japan's 'Price-Doubling' Plan?," *Asian Survey*, October 1965; Iwanami symposium, *Nihon Keizai Wa Do Naruka?*, esp. "Agaru Bukka" [Rising prices], pp. 74–92; R. Iochi, *Measurement of Consumer Price Changes by Income Classes* (Tokyo, 1964); S. Tsuru, "Business Cycles in Post-War Japan," in E. Lundberg, ed., *The Business Cycle in the Post-War World* (London, 1955); M. Shinohara, *Kodo Seicho No Himitsu* [The secret of accelerated growth], esp. Lecture 9, "Shotokubaizo To Bukkatoki" [Income-doubling and price rises]; T. Yoshino, ed., *Keizai Seicho To Bukka Mondai* [Economic growth and price problems] (Tokyo, 1962); Shimomura, "Seicho Seisaku No Kihon Mondai"; Shomomura, "9% No Seicho Ni Fuan Nashi" [The 9 percent growth rate without trepidation], *Economist* (Japan), October 17, 1961; Shimomura, "Consumer Price Problems," *Oriental Economist*, November and December 1963. Professor H. Ohuchi represents the extreme pessimistic view in the Iwanami symposium, while Dr. Shimomura will be found to represent the optimistic extreme in this price controversy in his article cited above.

THE EMPIRICAL BACKGROUND

During the post-surrender period from 1945 up to the 1948 Dodge disin-flationary monetary reform (including the stabilization of the Japanese yen at 360 to the dollar) Japan underwent a typical postwar hyperinflation as a result of acute general scarcity (which gave rise to a rampant black market) and an extraordinary pent-up demand supported by the government's massive rehabilitation outlays.[3] During the so-called Korean War boom from 1950 to 1953, Japan again experienced an inflation of the demand-pull variety because of the American-induced expansion of investment demand and con-sumption demand.[4] These two postwar inflations were due to exogenous causes—World War II and the Korean War—and therefore did not reflect the endogenous structure of the Japanese economy. After 1953, however, both wholesale and consumer prices continued to be fairly stable up to the announcement of the Income-Doubling Plan in 1960 and, to be more specific, before the unprecedented appearance of persistent labor shortages in 1959. Thereafter, the anomaly of continuously stable wholesale prices and rapidly rising consumer prices became the order of the day. A part of the effort in this chapter is to explain that coexistence in a way that might suggest prac-tical measures to make rapid growth compatible not only with price stability but also with general welfare.

Despite the rising trend of consumer prices, Japan managed to keep the rate of increase in general prices approximately equal to zero during the 1951–63 period,[5] while annually expanding its GNP by more than 9 percent in real terms on the average. In view of these facts, one might wonder what the recent inflation scare is all about unless one observed the peculiar Japanese political situation that makes welfare-geared, Marxian-oriented journalists and price-conscious neoclassical publicists strange bedfellows. More about this point later. By contrast, as recently as 1964, general prices were "more than doubling every year in Brazil and Indonesia, and rising at a rate which would result in their doubling in less than two years in the Congo, and every three years in Argentina, Chile, Colombia, Korea, and Uruguay."[6] This is a dramatic contrast indeed, but how does Japan's price behavior compare with that of other advanced industrial countries? Table 27 provides one answer, though it requires qualifying observations.

Let me make the following observations on the data given in the table. First, in all the industrial countries selected, both wholesale and consumer

---

[3] See my "Post-War Inflation and Fiscal-Monetary Policy of Japan," *American Economic Review*, December 1946. See also T. Kodera, "Post-War Inflation in Japan," *Kwansei Gakuin University Annual Studies*, August 1953.

[4] See Tsuru, "Business Cycles in Post-War Japan."

[5] See Eguchi, "Keizai Seicho To Tsuika Shinyo."

[6] Dorrance, "Inflation and Growth."

Table 27. International Price Differentials, 1964

Country	Wholesale Price Index*	Consumer Price Index*	Price Gap
Japan	144	191	47
Italy	118	165	47
U.K.	132	169	37
U.S.	115	129	14

SOURCE: adapted from the Iwanami symposium, Nihon Keizai Wa Do Naruka?, p. 85. The index figures are cited by Professor R. Minobe, who was a participant in that symposium, but he does not specify the sources of his data or his computational method. Compare the Ministry of International Trade and Industry's 1963 Sekai No Shohisha Bukka [The world's consumer prices].
*Base year, 1950.

prices were higher in 1964 than in 1950, thereby generally reflecting "inflation-biased," expansionary fiscal-monetary policies, full or near full employment cost pressures, the "administered pricing" of big business, the "countervailing" higher wage movements of organized labor, and, above all, increasing national money income relative to the short-period inelastic supply of goods and services in more or less rapidly growing economies. Second, Japan's high wholesale and consumer price indices for 1964 were, paradoxically, those of a recession year, thus reflecting the presence of pressures for higher prices amidst low general activity. However, it is noteworthy that Japan's real GNP increased by as much as 14 percent from 1963 to 1964, according to the Economic Planning Agency's 1965 White Paper. Third, the low U.S. price indices for 1964 seem to reflect the "tight-money" policies adopted because of increasing balance of payments difficulties, and they do not reflect the rising pressure of the Vietnam War on general domestic prices, which began making itself felt in 1965. Fourth, the relatively wide gap between the wholesale price indices and the consumer price indices for Japan, Italy, and the U.K. may reflect the low productivities of their consumer goods industries and service industries in comparison with productivities in those industries in the U.S. However, such productivity differentials among various sectors are inadequate to account for Japan's price gap fully. I shall return to this last point a little later. Last, the comparative levels of wholesale and consumer prices for any particular year for any country tell us nothing about the secular trend of general prices, which is most relevant to the relation of economic growth and price stability and which deserves far more attention than is commonly accorded it in discussions not only in Japan but elsewhere as well.

Let us pursue our inquiry into the aforementioned anomaly of stable wholesale prices with rising consumer prices by reference to Table 28. During the thirteen-year period 1950 to 1963 the wholesale price index remained

Table 28.   *Japanese Wholesale and Consumer Prices*

Year	Wholesale Price Index*	Consumer Price Index
1950	70.1	67.6
1951	97.3	78.7
1952	99.2	82.6
1953	99.9	88.0
1954	99.2	93.7
1955	97.4	92.7
1956	101.7	93.0
1957	104.8	95.9
1958	97.9	95.5
1959	98.9	96.5
1960	100.0	100.0
1961	101.0	105.3
1962	99.3	112.5
1963	101.1	121.0
1964	101.3	126.8
1965	102.1	135.1
1966	104.6	142.0
1967	106.5	147.7
1968	107.4	155.5

SOURCE: adapted from OECD's 1964 and 1969 *Economic Surveys: Japan.* The figures are based on Japanese statistical publications.
*Base year, 1960.

surprisingly stable, while the consumer price index steadily increased. Two matters need attention here, namely, the explanation of these radically different patterns of price behavior and their interpretation. These are highly controversial matters, as intimated at the outset of this chapter. Let me first suggest two separate yet related explanations for the stability of wholesale prices and galloping consumer prices.

Factors Making for the Stability of Wholesale Prices

1. The bulk of the items entering the wholesale price index are manufactures which are produced in increasingly efficient industries that enjoy economies of scale and hence low unit cost.

2. The power of big business in general to administer prices arbitrarily, particularly to prevent downward price flexibility even in the face of higher productivity which clearly warrants lowering of prices, is increasing.

3. Competition and uncertainty among oligopolistic industries is sufficient to induce those industries to adhere to mutually profitable price rigidity and,

instead, to engage in the advertising campaigns of product differentiation for larger shares of the market.

4. The productivity of labor is rising, more than offsetting higher money wages in the technologically advanced industries which do the most wholesale price-making, obviating the wage-price spiral in those industries.

5. Monetary-fiscal aids (in the form of long-term credits, subsidies, tax remissions, etc.) are highly selective, going to capacity-expanding producers of durable equipment rather than merely to demand-generating accumulators of inventories.

Factors Making for the Rising Trend in Consumer Prices

1. The greatest portion of the items entering the consumer price index is supplied by relatively inefficient agriculture (which requires the government's farm support policy and protection against imported foodstuffs), small-scale manufacturing industries, and service industries.

2. The productivity of labor lags far behind money wages in those industries supplying consumer goods and services, in recent years accompanied by a serious loss of labor to more efficient industries and by a consequential wage-equalization tendency.

3. Overlapping small retail stores with highly inefficient marketing and distributing techniques (supermarkets, department stores, and long-distance trucking and hauling are not yet so widespread in Japan as in America) are preponderant.

4. The monopolistic downward rigidity of wholesale prices prevents retail and consumer prices from falling significantly even during a recession.

5. Consumer demand, based on rising per capita national income, for better food, clothing, shelter, household gadgets, and services increases relative to their supply, which is diminished by the growth-induced allocation of resources to capital goods and export industries.

These two sets of factors will probably describe the behavior of Japanese wholesale and consumer prices in the decades ahead in the absence of radical changes in the prevailing technological-institutional complex or in monetary-fiscal policy. At any rate, they require hypothesis-testing by Japanese econometricians not only for the 1950–63 period but for the future. With this postscript, let us turn to some relevant implications.

Implications of Japanese Patterns of Price Behavior

1. Persistently stable wholesale prices are conducive to export expansion, provided (a) that the rest of the world has a more than unitary elasticity of demand for imports from Japan with respect to both price and income, and (b) that "quality competition" does not supersede "price competition" in the world market as well as in domestic markets.

2. The secular stability of wholesale prices is a decisive counterweight to the rising trend of consumer prices and would help Japan to sustain general price stability *pari passu* with rapid economic growth, albeit less satisfactorily than if consumer prices were also persistently stable.

3. The continuing stability of wholesale prices would enable Japan's policymakers to concentrate on measures to stabilize consumer prices in order to justify their professed goals of welfare, stability, and growth.

4. The continuity of stable wholesale prices would help to reduce that uncertainty about profit expectations which hinders investment in durable equipment, and so would contribute to growth of capacity relative to expansion of demand.

5. The stability of wholesale prices, when coexisting anomalously with rising consumer prices, is a rather unfavorable commentary on the onesidedness of Japan's inflation-biased, sound-finance-minded monetary-fiscal policies and its balance of payments-inspired deflationary statecraft, with little regard to consumer welfare.

6. The rising trend of consumer prices has the negative virtue of serving as a warning to the inefficient supplier of consumer goods and services as well as against administered downward rigidity of wholesale prices affecting retail and consumer prices.

7. Steadily rising consumer prices would court the danger of increasing such consumer resistance as to cause serious excess capacity in consumer goods industries and eventually in capital goods industries.

8. The upward instability of consumer prices would make wage earners, who do the most consuming, so real income-conscious as to demand escalator clauses in their labor contracts and other cost-of-living adjustments that could only strengthen the entrepreneurial belief in the supposed "necessity" of administered price hikes at the wholesale level.

9. Low-income consumers, who spend most of their incomes on food, clothing, and shelter, would bear the brunt of rising consumer prices and so might be provoked into adding fuel to the socio-political fire of perverse "anti-inflation obscurantism" and understandable yet fruitless spoon-rattling housewives' protests against individual retail "profiteers" charging higher grocery prices (known in Japan as *shamoji-undo*).

10. Failure to arrest rising consumer prices permanently, instead of temporarily, would give substance to the charge that capitalism cannot grow except by exploiting wage earners who make up the bulk of the consuming public, lip-service to "mass welfare" notwithstanding.

Such are the implications of the uneasy coexistence of stable wholesale prices and rising consumer prices in the growing Japanese economy as I see it. Let us now look at the secular trend of general prices. Table 29 shows that Japan's general prices, while fluctuating cyclically in semilogarithmic terms, nevertheless increased at an approximately zero rate of change during the 1951-63 period, for the sum of positive and negative rates of change in

Table 29. *Rates of Change in General Prices, 1951–63*

Year	Rate of Change
1951	.139
1952	-.167
1953	.066
1954	-.059
1955	-.024
1956	.061
1957	-.030
1958	-.037
1959	.051
1960	-.004
1961	.025
1962	-.025
1963	.013

SOURCE: adapted from Eguchi, "Keizai Seicho To Tsuika Shinyo." Here the rate of change in general prices is given by the formula

$$\frac{\Delta p}{p} = \frac{p_t - p_{t-1}}{p_{t-1}} = 0,$$

where p is the index of general prices, t is the current period, and $t-1$ is the preceding period.

general prices over that period comes to approximately zero, the positive and negative values roughly canceling each other out. This is a remarkable achievement, especially in view of the rising trend of consumer prices noted above. Such an achievement in the rapidly growing Japanese economy is of great didactic significance to present-day developing economies confronted with persistent inflationary pressures, for reasons to be explored in the next section. It is of particular importance to the Japanese economy's own progress in terms of expanding real national income, for a low rate of increase in general prices implies a low deflator for calculating real GNP from any given nominal GNP. The Japanese Economic Planning Agency's projected rate of growth of real GNP for 1970 could not be as high as 7.2 percent unless, among other things, it did not confidently anticipate secular stability of general prices with a positive but small average annual rate of increase. We shall see in the next section just what rate of increase of general prices is likely to be compatible with the given target rate of growth of real GNP. Table 29 also serves as a salutary dampener on anti-inflation hysteria.

Mr. T. Eguchi, on whose data Table 29 is based, has provided additional data for the prewar and immediate postwar periods and so has given us a graphic picture of the long-run behavior of the rate of change in Japanese general prices from 1936 to 1963. With his permission, I reproduce his diagram in the slightly more rigorous manner shown in the figure. The figure reveals that general prices increased at a positive but small constant rate in Japan, as well as elsewhere, during the 1936-44 period, which includes the impact of the Great Depression and of World War II, at an abnormal hyperinflationary rate during the immediate postwar period (from about 1945 to 1948), moved sharply downward to a negative figure (with the largest amplitude, max g^p - min g^p, in the recent history of the Japanese economy), and showed an approximately zero trend during the 1951-63 period. It clearly reflects the changing effectiveness of price stabilization policies, exogenous influences of an unforeseen nature (i.e., wars), the cyclical vagaries of general economic activity, and endogenous influences of a structural nature. That portion of the figure which covers the period 1950-63 supports the view that recently rising consumer prices cannot and must not be exaggerated into an overall inflation, however painful and regrettable those price increases may be in themselves. This does not, of course, mean that the Japanese economy can afford to remain indifferent to the rising trend of consumer prices. But it

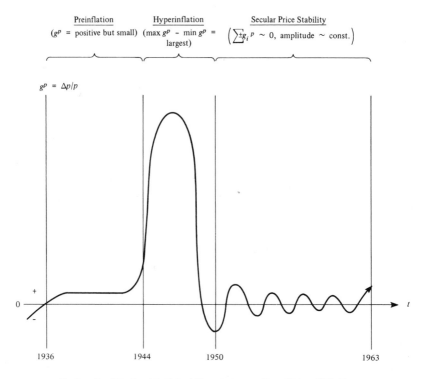

The Long-Run Behavior of the Rate of Change in Japanese General Prices, 1936-63.

does mean that one should be careful not to commit a "fallacy of composition" on this score, as well as on other micro-macro issues.

CONDITIONS FOR RAPID GROWTH WITHOUT SECULAR INFLATION

Japan's recent inflation-deflation muddle cannot be disentangled by rhetoric, invective, or even by price stabilization measures without sound theoretical foundations. As noted earlier, Dr. O. Shimomura has gone to the one extreme of understating the possible danger of secular inflation that is latent in an overambitious growing economy, while Professor H. Ohuchi has gone to the other extreme of overstating the rising trend of consumer prices so as to advocate the abandonment of what he regards as a price-doubling plot. Both these men, while undoubtedly concerned with the national goal of making growth and welfare compatible, nevertheless have failed to justify their diametrically opposed positions in an operationally significant and cogent way.

A rare exception to this extreme tendency can be seen in the recent writing of Mr. Eguchi mentioned above. The essence of his argument is that if the Japanese economy's capital productivity is technologically increased or if its voluntary savings ratio is somehow increased in the future, there will be so much less need for credit-financed investment that the rate of increase in general prices will drop without sacrificing rapid growth. He justifies his conclusion through the econometric extrapolation of the past trend within the general framework of the Harrod-Domar growth model. However, Mr. Eguchi's model suffers from undue vagueness concerning the demand and supply sides of the growing Japanese economy: it does not fully analyze Domar's "dual character of investment" affecting the income-generating and capacity-expanding aspects of investment relative to secular price behavior. Nor does his model take into account such implications of secular inflation for income distribution as Professor M. Bronfenbrenner has analyzed.[7]

General Prices and Rapid Growth

By way of avoiding the "anti-inflation obscurantism," intentional or otherwise, which militates against full employment and rapid growth, I propose to build an alternative model to illustrate the technical relation of growth and inflation, with a view to indicating conditions that need to be satisfied for achieving rapid growth without secular price instability:

$$(1.1) \quad \Delta Y^m = \Delta C^m + \Delta I^m = (1 - s^m)\Delta Y^m + \Delta I^m \quad (\Delta I^m / Y^m = i)$$

---

[7]See M. Bronfenbrenner, "Some Neglected Implications of Secular Inflation," in K. Kurihara, ed., *Post Keynesian Economics* (New Brunswick, N.J., 1954).

where Y^m is national money income, C^m is money consumption expenditure, I^m is money investment of the autonomous variety, s^m is the marginal propensity to save out of national money income, and i is the ratio of additional autonomous money investment to national money income. From (1.1), including the indicator, we get

$$(1.2) \quad g^m \equiv \frac{\Delta Y^m}{Y^m} = \frac{i}{s^m} \qquad \text{(rate of growth of national money income)}$$

which shows the possibility that national money income may vary directly with i and inversely with s^m. This g^m given by (1.2) represents the demand side of a growing economy, and includes in the independent variable i such impacts of credit-financed investment as Mr. Eguchi discusses.

$$(1.3) \quad \Delta Y^r = \sigma I^r \qquad (I^r/Y^r = S^r/Y^r \equiv s^r)$$

where Y^r is real national income, I^r ($\equiv \Delta K$) is autonomous net investment in real terms (identical with an addition to the capital stock), S^r is savings out of real national income, σ is capital productivity, and s^r is the average propensity to save out of real national income. Here it is assumed, as shown parenthetically, that the investment ratio (I^r/Y^r) is, in equilibrium, equal to the savings ratio (S^r/Y^r). From (1.3), including the indicator, we derive

$$(1.4) \quad g^r \equiv \frac{\Delta Y^r}{Y^r} = \sigma s^r \qquad \text{(rate of growth of real national income)}$$

which shows the possibility that real national income may vary in direct proportion to changes in σ and s^r. This g^r given by (1.4) represents the supply side of a growing economy, and also includes credit-financed investment in the independent variable s^r (via $I^r/Y^r = S^r/Y^r$).

The rate of growth of national money income and the rate of growth of real national income determined by (1.1)–(1.4) will be found, between them, to determine the rate of increase in general prices. To show such a causal relation in the context of a growing economy, it is necessary to dynamize Y^m and Y^r in the following exponential equations:

$$(1.5) \quad Y^m(0) = p(0)Y^r(0)$$
$$(1.6) \quad Y^m(t) = p(t)Y^r(t)$$
$$(1.7) \quad Y^r(t) = Y^r(0)(1 + \sigma s^r)^t = Y^r(0)(1 + g^r)^t$$
$$(1.8) \quad p(t) = p(0)(1 + g^p)^t \qquad (g^p \equiv \Delta p/p)$$
$$(1.9) \quad Y^m(t) = Y^m(0)[1 + (i/s^m)]^t = Y^m(0)(1 + g^m)^t$$

$$(1.10) \quad g^m \equiv \frac{Y^m(t)}{Y^m(0)} - 1 = \frac{p(0)(1 + g^p)Y^r(0)(1 + g^r)}{p(0)Y^r(0)} - 1$$

$$= (1 + g^p)(1 + g^r) - 1$$

$$(1.11) \quad \frac{\Delta p}{p} \equiv g^p = \frac{1 + g^m}{1 + g^r} - 1 \quad \text{(rate of increase in general prices)}$$

Here p is the index of general prices, g^p is the average annual rate of increase in general prices, and t is time, while $p(0)$, $Y^r(0)$, and $Y^m(0)$ are the initial values of these variables. Equation (1.11), derived from (1.5)-(1.10), shows that the rate of increase in general prices is capable of varying directly with the rate of growth of national money income and inversely with the rate of growth of real national income. It carries with it the implication that an economy whose demand and supply sides are both growing (rather than only the demand side when output is completely inelastic with respect to expenditure in short-period conditions of full employment) must satisfy the condition of general price equilibrium in terms of ratios, if there is to be secular price stability:

$$(1.12) \quad g^m = g^r; \quad \frac{i}{s^m} - \sigma s^r = 0 \quad \text{(condition for secular price stability)}$$

We may generalize (1.5)-(1.12) thus: if $g^m - g^r = 0$, then $g^p = 0$ (secular price stability); if $g^m - g^r > 0$, then $g^p > 0$ (upward price trend); if $g^m - g^r < 0$, then $g^p < 0$ (downward price trend). These stylized generalizations can be further implemented by the hypothetical numerical model of Table 30, which indicates that, in an economy whose effective demand (expressed in g^m) and productive capacity (expressed in g^r) are both expanding over time, the initial price stability of some base period can be restored at some future time $(t + n)$, and at the higher balanced growth rate at that $[g^m(t + n) = g^r(t + n); g^p(t + n) = 0$, and $g^m(t + n), g^r(t + n) > g^m(t), g^r(t)$, when $t = 0, 1, 2, \ldots, n]$. This means, in terms of policy operations, that the fiscal-monetary authorities of the economy in question would have to exercise a guiding influence on the secular behavior of i and s^m affecting the demand side (g^m) while simultaneously influencing that of r^r and σ affecting the supply side (g^r) if they are to help achieve balanced growth without secular inflation $[g^m(t) = g^r(t); g^p(t) = 0]$.

Thus Table 30 strongly suggests the theoretical desirability of fighting secular inflation on two fronts, that is, on the demand and supply sides at the same time, even though a short-period anti-inflationary or disinflationary

Table 30.   Hypothetical Secular Price Behavior

$g^m(t)$	$g^r(t)$	$g^p(t) = \dfrac{1 + g^m(t)}{1 + g^r(t)} - 1$
0.05	0.05	0.000 (initial price stability)
0.08	0.06	0.018 (upward price instability)
0.10	0.12	−0.012 (downward price instability)
0.13	0.13	0.000 (eventual price stability)

policy on the demand side alone is admittedly an easier political expedient. It also warns would-be "anti-inflation" obscurantists and alarmists that deficit financing, long-term credit extensions to investors in fixed capital, and other fiscal-monetary measures to stimulate the private inducement to invest must be judged conducive to secular inflation by due reference to those trend forces affecting s^m relative to i on the demand side of a growing economy and σ relative to s^r on the supply side.

Consumer Prices in a Cost-Push Economy

Given near-full or full employment expansion of effective demand, the preponderance of unproductive service industries, government-protected marginal agriculture, increasing shortages of labor, the interindustry wage-equalization tendency, and the oligopolistic downward rigidity of prices of consumer durables, the stage is set for rising consumer prices. The preceding chapters have shown the whys and hows of these structural characteristics of the rapidly growing Japanese economy. It is therefore little wonder that Japan should be confronted with the anomaly of rising consumer prices coexisting with stable wholesale prices. However, the Japanese economy is by no means alone in this paradoxical experience, for other advanced industrial economies are also experiencing similar price phenomena and trends. This means that the danger of so-called cost-push inflation is difficult to avoid in the industrially advanced economies, though it can be minimized by deliberate adjustments among the cost-push elements of a multisectoral growing economy. Neither the foes of rising consumer prices nor the friends of consumer price stabilization (both in Japan and elsewhere) seem to go much farther than simply to put all the blame on organized labor's demands for higher wages or, to a lesser extent, on price-administering big business.

If rising consumer prices of a persistent nature were left uncontrolled simply because wholesale prices remained stable, as Dr. O. Shimomura and other optimists seem to advocate, the Japanese economy's general price index would not exhibit in the future such a remarkable degree of secular stability as it has in the past, to the detriment of both consumer welfare and overall growth. The recently expressed concern of the Japanese Economic Planning Agency about the rising trend of consumer prices (in its 1965 White Paper on stable growth) is an opportune and promising commentary on Japan's price stabilization policy. As early as 1961, Professor M. Shinohara suggested that rising consumer prices should and could be halted by appropriate structural adjustments, such as the increasing substitution of labor-saving gadgets for labor-expending services by households and raising of productivity in manufacturing industries and agriculture in order to lower the prices of consumer durables and other consumer goods.[8] This interesting suggestion, however, ignores both the intrinsically labor-intensive nature of service industries, which defy extensive automation, and the institutionally established power of big business to maintain higher prices, which disobeys the competitive micro price law ($p = AR = MR = MC$, where p is the price of any good, AR is average revenue, MR is marginal revenue, and MC is marginal cost), let alone the artificially supported prices of agricultural produce. Nevertheless, Professor Shinohara's prescription does point up the importance of studying the structures of productivity, cost, and demand as they affect the rising trend of consumer prices.

Professor S. Ozaki has recently suggested such antidotes to rising consumer prices as increased productivity in agriculture, service industries, and small business enterprises, more stringent public control of oligopolistic industries and labor unions, and the elimination of protective tariffs against imported foodstuffs.[9] He shows a greater awareness of the institutional and political factors affecting rising consumer prices of a cost-push nature than does Professor Shinohara, though they share the goal of increased productivity in some sectors. However, Professor Ozaki is no less vague than Professor Shinohara concerning the technical relation of consumer prices and cost-push variables implied by his policy suggestions. It is noteworthy that neither Professor Shinohara nor Professor Ozaki advocates an overall deflationary policy for the sake of consumer price stability but at the risk of jeopardizing attainment of full employment.

By contrast, Professor Ohuchi, whose pessimistic forecast of rising consumer prices is as extreme as Dr. Shimomura's optimistic view, has vehemently attacked Keynes and other "bourgeois" economists as harboring and supporting an essentially "anti-masses" inflationary economy and really "unstable" growth, their references to the goal of "stable accelerated growth" notwithstanding.[10] This attitude is not unlike that of Professor F. Machlup, who lumps together interventionists, socialists, et al., in the category of "inflationists," as the reader of his "The Finance of Development in Poor

[8] Shinohara, *Kodo Seicho No Himitsu*, p. 138.
[9] Ozaki, "Japan's 'Price-Doubling' Plan?."
[10] Compare the Iwanami symposium, *Nihon Keizai Wa Do Naruka?*, pp. 87–88.

Countries: Foreign Capital and Domestic Inflation" in the April 1956 issue of
Riron Keizaigaku will recall. Mr. Eguchi, after having established the secular
stability of general prices over the 1950–63 period and as if to answer such
anti-inflationists as Professors Ohuchi and Machlup, dryly remarks that such
"theories" as would characterize the Japanese economy since 1960 or 1961
(the steadily rising consumer price trend coinciding with the beginning of the
Income-Doubling Plan) as "inflationary" can only be regarded as politically
motivated or as common hearsays. [11]

So much for critical observations on Japan's consumer price controversy.
Let me turn to more analytical aspects of the problem in hand. To clarify the
nature and direction of cost changes making for cost-push inflation, the
following general model[12] may be useful:

$$(2.1) \quad pY = wN + (\pi + r)qK$$

where Y is national output, N is labor input, K is capital input, p is the
general price index, g is the unit price of capital input, w is the average money
wage rate, π is the average net profit rate, and r is the rate of interest. Here
pY is equivalent to national money income, wN to total wage income, and
$(\pi + r)qK$ to total profit income (subsuming rent and other property
incomes). Equation (2.1) simply tells us that national money income must, in
equilibrium, equal the sum of the respective shares of wage earners and profit-
takers, but it also contains helpful information about certain relevant
cost-push elements affecting the behavior of general prices.

Dividing both sides of equation (2.1) by Y yields

$$(2.2) \quad p = \frac{WN + (\pi + r)gK}{Y}$$

the numerator and denominator of the righthand side of which equation can
be divided by N while letting $K/N \equiv \theta$ and $Y/N \equiv \rho$, so as to give

$$(2.3) \quad p = \frac{w + (\pi + r)q\theta}{\rho}$$

where θ is the capital-labor ratio and ρ is the average productivity of labor,
and where the numerator $w + (\pi + r)q\theta$ represents the cost structure.
Equation (2.3) has as its independent variables efficiency wage rate w/ρ, the
supply price of capital $(\pi + r)q$, and the degree of capital intensity θ. The
money wage rate w relative to labor productivity ρ is the most important

---

[11] Eguchi, "Keizai Seicho To Tsuika Shinyo."
[12] This is a slightly modified version of my earlier model in *National Income and Economic
Growth*.

single determinant of general prices from the standpoint of the cost structure. The supply price of capital $(\pi + r)q$ is made up of the net profit rate (π) measuring the real cost of risk and uncertainty involved in the normal utilization of capital, the interest rate (r) measuring the cost of money (capital charges), and the unit price of capital input (q) measuring the replacement cost of capital. All these cost variables are subject to autonomous manipulation quite independent of market forces.

The price level determined in a manner shown by (2.3) may rise exponentially according to

$$(2.4) \quad p_t = p_0(1 + g^p)^t; \quad \frac{p^t}{p_0} - 1 = g^p \quad (t = 0, 1)$$

where g^p is the average annual rate of increase in general prices and t is time. Taking equation (2.3) into account, we can express the rate of growth of cost-push inflation (g^p) involved in equation (2.4) as

$$(2.5) \quad g^p = \frac{p_t}{p_0} - 1 = \frac{[w_t + (\pi_t + r_t)q_t\theta_t]/\rho_t}{[w_0 + (\pi_0 + r_0)q_0\theta_0]/\rho_t} - 1$$

Equation (2.5) indicates the possibility that the rate of growth of cost-push inflation is positive, negative, or zero depending on the technical relation of the current values of the independent variables (at time 1) and the initial values of those variables (at time 0). It also implies that the general price level given by equation (2.3) would have to be estimated at a given point of time by reference to the cost and technological variables regarded as flexible structural parameters.

Applied to the Japanese economy, p given by (2.3) might be thought of as representing the index of consumer prices, and then w, π, r, q, θ, and ρ might be interpreted as representing the cost-productivity structure of consumer goods and service industries (primary, secondary, and tertiary sectors supplying consumer goods and services). Thus viewed, the prevailing or future trend of consumer prices can be estimated by observing or anticipating the dynamic behavior of those independent variables in the specific context of the growing Japanese economy. Subject to econometric testing, I venture to offer some hypotheses regarding the future behavior of those variables.

1. The money wage (w) will rise, partly because of general full employment conditions, partly because of specific labor shortages in consumer goods and service industries, partly because of "countervailing" higher wage movements of organized labor in those industries, and partly because of the increasing demand for consumer goods and services and the correspondingly increasing derived demand for labor.

2. The net profit rate (k) will rise, partly because the real cost of risk and uncertainty in small businesses supplying most consumer goods and services is subjectively greater than in large ones mainly supplying capital goods, but largely because larger suppliers of increasingly demanded consumer durables are usually addicted to maintaining a higher than average "target rate of return" on investment as a desideratum for prestige, expansion, and other long-run reasons.

3. The interest rate (r) will be kept high, if it does not rise significantly, largely because the interest elasticity of investment is generally very low in the Japanese economy, especially in persistently booming conditions that promise higher and higher levels of the marginal efficiency of capital.

4. The unit price of capital input (q) will rise (as in America, where attempts have recently been made by big producers of raw steel, aluminum, and copper to increase their prices arbitrarily so as to threaten widespread repercussions on the consumer prices of automobiles and other consumer durables dependent on those capital inputs), largely because of the "administered-pricing" policies of large suppliers of raw materials and other inputs entering consumer goods industries.

5. The capital-labor ratio (θ) will remain more or less stable, attempts to substitute capital for labor in labor-scarce consumer goods and service industries being frustrated not only by higher prices of labor inputs but also by the increasing elasticity of employment (demand for labor) in the tertiary sector of the economy.

6. Labor productivity (ρ) will also remain more or less stable, largely because technological progress in consumer goods and service industries as a whole (with the notable exception of transportation and communications) is likely to remain much slower than that in most capital goods industries, and partly because agriculture and most services in Japan defy extensive mechanization and rationalization.

On these hypotheses and according to equation (2.3), consumer prices are likely to increase secularly in the future growing Japanese economy, that is, in the absence of deliberate counterbalancing measures to influence the secular behavior of w, π, r, q, θ, and ρ. Equation (2.5) carries with it the policy implication that Japanese policymakers would have to adopt such institutional-technological courses of action as to make for $(p_t/p_0) - 1 = g^p = 0$. The earlier catalogue of the factors making for the rising trend of consumer prices, together with the above hypotheses, suggests, I believe, concrete practical measures to stabilize consumer prices in the Japanese economy and so to render stable growth without secular inflation of any kind ("demand-pull" or "cost-push") feasible. Only then will the professed goal of stable growth cease to be an empty slogan and begin to make for the compatibility of growth and welfare.

CHAPTER TEN

THE BALANCE OF PAYMENTS
AND SUSTAINED GROWTH

Ex ante maintenance of the balance of payments equilibrium is considered a *sine qua non* of sustained growth in the postwar Japanese economy, for four broad reasons. First, the goal of "stable growth" includes external equilibrium as well as internal price stability. Second, recurrent balance of payments crises would give rise to such frequent deflationary policies as might seriously weaken the country's long-run growth potential. Third, the rising demand for imports because of the greater raw material needs of expanding industries, higher domestic income, and import liberalization all round would necessitate matching exports if a persistent deficit on capital account is to be avoided. Fourth, the relentless discipline of striving for a balance of payments equilibrium against tremendous odds would exercise a salutary influence on domestic structural adjustments along the lines of comparative advantage and stable growth. This chapter will examine these broadly conceived notions both empirically and analytically, with a view to throwing additional light on the relationship of foreign trade and economic growth, a relationship which has stirred a great and continuing debate among Japanese economists and policymakers in the past decade or so.[1] Specifically, I shall discuss in this chapter the shifting pattern of Japanese foreign trade and illustrative models of trade and growth in the Japanese context.

[1] See Shinohara, *Kodo Seicho No Himitsu*, esp. Lectures 2 and 3, and "Economic Development and Foreign Trade in Pre-War Japan" (including postwar material), in Cowan, ed., *The Economic Development of China and Japan*; S. Tsuru, "Variations in the Foreign-Exchange Rate" (in Japanese), *Shukan Asahi* [Asahi Weekly], May 30, 1954; T. Kodera, *Kokusai Tsukaron* [International currency theory], 1957; S. Ichimura, *Nihon Keizai No Kozo* [The structure of the Japanese economy] (Tokyo, 1957), esp. chap. 9; K. Kojima, ed., *Ronso: Keizai Seicho To Nihon Boeki* [Debate: economic growth and Japanese foreign trade] (Tokyo, 1960); H. Kanamori, "Yagate Antei Seicho No Kodoe" [Toward a stable growth path], in *Japan Economic Research Center Monthly Report*, September 1965; K. Nagashima, "Economic Projection under the International Circumstances," *Bulletin of University of Osaka Prefecture*, 6 (1962); Nakayama, ed., *Nihon Keizai No Seicho*, pp. 174–211; Iwanami symposium, *Nihon Keizai Wa Do Naruka?*, pp. 116–31; Japan Committee for Economic Development, "A Statement of National Policy," in CED, *Japan in the Free World Economy*; Federation of Economic Organizations, *Japan Striving for Better Global Co-operation*, esp. chap. 3; O. Shimomura, "Keizai Seisaku No Ninmu To

THE SHIFTING PATTERN OF FOREIGN TRADE

Before taking up an empirical investigation, some general remarks on the place of exports and imports in the overall balance of payments may be useful. Exports and imports on current account are by far the most important determinant of a trading nation's balance of payments position; in other words, it is the balance of trade which is of greatest analytical significance to the balance of payments equilibrium or disequilibrium in the long run, since it reflects the structural abilities of a trading nation to produce and export goods and services relative to its structural needs for imported additions to national output. By contrast, it is export variations relative to the constant marginal import ratio which figure importantly in the short-run foreign-trade multiplier analysis. This analytical contrast has been stressed by no less than Sir Roy Harrod,[2] the celebrated author of *International Economics* and *Towards a Dynamic Economics*.

Moreover, it is a positive balance of current transactions (an export surplus, visible and invisible) which enables an industrially advanced trading nation not only to obviate a negative balance of capital transactions (to finance an import surplus) but also to maintain its lending status (creditor position) for its own future overseas earnings as well as for the immediate provision of financial assistance to economically less advanced nations. By contrast, it is a negative balance of capital transactions (net foreign borrowing) which enables a present-day developing nation not only to minimize national belt-tightening but also to take advantage of its borrowing stage without the traditional fear of "political strings" or "repayment problems" (unless the proceeds of foreign borrowing are wasted on unproductive projects or the terms of lending preclude a liberal interest and amortization provision).

As far as the Japanese economy of today is concerned,[3] it is a surplus in visible trade which is most needed to offset a deficit in invisible trade as well as in short-term capital transactions. Since Japan is more often than not a net lender in long-term capital transactions nowadays, Mr. Colin Clark's inclusion of that country among high-saving and, by implication, creditor nations is by and large justified.[4] Be that as it may, the main point to be noted here is that,

---

Sekinin" [The duty and responsibility of economic policy], *Japan Economic Research Center Monthly Report*, September 1965; Ministry of International Trade and Industry, *Tsusho Hakusho* [White Paper on foreign commerce] (Tokyo, 1963 and 1965); Oriental Economist, *Japan Economic Yearbook*.

[2] See his *Towards a Dynamic Economics* (esp. Lecture 4, "The Foreign Balance").

[3] For earlier postwar trade conditions, see my "Japan's Trade Position in a Changing World Market," *Review of Economics and Statistics*, November 1955.

[4] C. Clark, "The World Will Save Money in the 1950's," *Fortune*, July 1950. As a member of the OECD and a signatory to the Colombo Plan, Japan is committed to a national policy of extending greater financial and technical assistance to the less developed nations in the future.

under the present circumstances, Japan's balance of payments problem boils
down to one of making exports grow faster than imports within technical
limits (price-income elasticities of exports and imports, the IMF limitation on
exchange-rate depreciation, the General Agreement on Tariffs and Trade
regulations, etc.).

So much for the a priori preliminaries. Let us turn to a posteriori observations. The balance of payments statement in Table 31 serves as a convenient
starting point. In the table the current transactions balance column records
the net results of visible and invisible trade balances and transfer accounts,
while the overall balance column includes long-term and short-term capital
balances. Since the transfer account for the 1961-68 period remained fairly
constant, the current transactions balance for that period largely reflects the
trend difference between exports and imports. The 1968 level of foreign
exchange reserves amounted to $3,213 million, which would hardly support
Japan's imports for four months if these imports continued at the annual rate

Table 31.   Japan's Balance of Payments, 1961-68

Fiscal Year	Current Transactions Balance*	Overall Balance*	Foreign Exchange Reserve*
1961	-1,015	-855	1,741
1962	16	281	2,043
1963	-1,071	-360	1,996
1964	28	106	2,053
1965	1,048	428	2,109
1966	994	58	2,077
1967	-313	-535	1,963
1968	1,530	1,627	3,213

SOURCE: adapted from Oriental Economist, *Japan Economic Yearbook* (Tokyo, 1969), pp.
72-73.
*In millions of current dollars.

of $10,443 million as specified in the *Japan Economic Yearbook*). Such a
precarious foreign exchange reserve situation would require more exports and
less imports, as well as a larger surplus in long-term capital transactions than
in the past, for a greater margin of safety in Japan's external payments
position. Yet none of these requirements is likely to be instituted, nor can
they quickly be met, for reasons to be explored.

This brings us to the consideration of Japan's import dependence. Table
32 tells an interesting story about Japan's changing import dependence in a

---

See the Ministry of International Trade and Industry's 1965 White Paper on foreign commerce.
Japan has actually turned into a creditor nation since January 1967, according to *Nihon Keizai
Shinbun* [Japanese Economic Press], March 12, 1967.

Table 32. Japan's Changing Import Dependence

Period	Overall Import Ratio	Specific Import Ratio					
		Food	Fuel	Metals and machines	Chemicals	Textiles	Rubber and hides
1926-39	21.0%						
1946-52	7.9%						
1953-58	15.0%	3.0%	1.7%	6.0%	7.0%	26.6%	28.2%
1963-68	10.33%						

*The figures for the 1926-58 period are adapted from Nakayama, ed., *Nihon Kaizai No Seicho*, pp. 175-81. The "import ratio" in that period is equal to merchandise imports divided by GNP in terms of 1934-36 constant prices. The average import ratio for the 1963-68 period is calculated on the basis of 1965 constant prices and is based on OECD, *Economic Surveys: Japan*, p. 46.

changing world and over a long span of more than three decades from the prewar year of 1926 to the postwar year of 1958. During the 1926-39 period, which includes the years of the Great Depression, Japan's overall import ratio was as high as shown here largely because of the slow growth of those industries which should have but did not emerge with import-substituting techniques (e.g., synthetic fibers, plastics, and transistorization) and partly because of the relatively high level of exports which that country was able to maintain, despite the Great Depression, through the worsened terms of trade and currency depreciation.[5] The extremely low figure of 7.9 percent for the immediate postwar period is an obvious reflection of a defeated Japan's temporary inability to earn import-paying foreign exchange through its own exports in the then hostile world market; the figure would have been much smaller had it not been for American aid and credits. The figure of 15 percent for the 1953-58 postindependence period, while far below the prewar level, nevertheless is a highly favorable commentary on Japan's more recent efforts to reduce its traditional dependence on imported industrial raw materials, to increase self-sufficiency in food production, and to expand the domestic production of relatively low-priced consumer durables (e.g., automobiles, refrigerators, and washing machines). The figure for the 1963-68 period is strongly suggestive of Japan's import-substituting industrialization trend in recent years.

The specific import ratios for the 1953-58 period are not in themselves capable of showing an upward or downward trend unless and until we examine the relative weight of the import-dependent sectoral outputs in total

[5] For the latter reasons, see Shinohara, "Economic Development and Foreign Trade in Pre-War Japan."

industrial production. Available data[6] reveal that, for the same period, the output of the rubber-hides sector with its 28 percent import ratio constituted only 3.2 percent of total industrial output and that of the textiles sector with its 26.6 percent import ratio constituted 14.9 percent of total industrial output. On the other hand, the output of the metals-machines sector with a 6 percent import ratio represented as much as 48.6 percent of total industrial output, while that of the chemicals sector with a 7 percent import ratio represented 25.2 percent of that total.

In the light of these sectoral comparisons we may speculate on the future trend of the overall import ratio. Owing to the declining relative importance of the textile and other heavily import-dependent sectors for Japan's total industrial production and to the rising relative importance of the machine and other much less import-dependent sectors, the ratio of imported raw materials to national output is likely to show a downward trend. Since raw materials make up the bulk of Japanese imports, the presumption is that the overall import ratio will show a downward trend in the future. However, the true overall import ratio would have to be computed by including invisible imports. Japanese trade statistics indicate a definitely rising trend of invisible imports in recent years, implying an upward pressure on the overall import ratio. Moreover, there are such other upward pressures on the overall import ratio as the increasing need for imported oil (incident to the postwar "energy revolution"), the rising propensity to spend on more and better consumer goods, including foreign ones (which, if imported, would appear relatively attractive in comparison with high-priced domestic ones), and the gradual liberalization of import restrictions all around.

Dr. O. Shimomura's recent estimate of a 9 percent import ratio for the Japanese economy,[7] which is considerably lower than the 1953–58 average figure of 15 percent, may be in part the result of his pious hope for import-substituting technological progress, in part the result of his optimistic statistical biases. Professor S. Tsuru emphasizes the desirability of regarding the import ratio as a manipulative policy parameter rather than as a fixed coefficient.[8] He implies that it is better to adjust the import ratio to whatever target rate of growth is deemed necessary than to speculate on the upward or downward future trend of that ratio. I find myself agreeing with Professor Tsuru on this score. Professor S. Ichimura has called attention to the rising imports of foodstuffs in recent years as possibly putting an upward pressure on the *ex post* stability of the import ratio around the average figure of 12 or 13 percent.[9] If the Japanese economy succeeds in stabilizing the import ratio

[6] See Nakayama, ed., *Nihon Keizai No Seicho*, p. 181.
[7] Shimomura, "Keizai Seisaku No Ninmu To Sekinin."
[8] Tsuru, in Nakayama, ed., *Nihon Keizai No Seicho*, p. 203.
[9] Ichimura, *The Japanese Economy in the World*, p. 146.

at the secular level of 10 percent or less, the "export or expire" drive can be more relaxed in the future than in the past.

Let us turn to the discussion of the export side. Table 33 shows a striking development seen in the preponderant exportation of heavy industry products in the ten-year postwar period 1953 to 1963. Exports of chemicals, metal manufactures, and machines rose to six to nine times the 1953 level,

Table 33. *The Changing Composition of Japan's Exports, 1953–63*

Export Item	Export Volume Index*
Light industry:	
foodstuffs	228.8
textiles	285.0
non-ferrous products	322.1
Heavy industry:	
chemicals	759.4
metal manufactures	615.3
machines	901.4
Others	557.9

SOURCE: adapted from 1963 *Honbo Keizai Tokei* [Yearbook of economic statistics] (Tokyo, 1963).
*Base year, 1953.

whereas exports of such traditional light industry products as textiles, foodstuffs, and non-ferrous products rose to only two to three times the 1953 level. These changes in the composition of postwar Japan's exports reflect not only a radical shift to heavy industry for rapid growth but also other trading countries' increasing demand for heavy industry products. Of those heavy industry products exported, radios (especially transistors), motor vehicles (including automobiles, motorcycles, tractors, and trucks), optical instruments, and synthetic fiber fabrics are new items which have made noteworthy progress since the end of Pacific hostilities. This changing composition of Japan's exports makes for stable growth because the greater production of heavy industry products strengthens the country's growth potential and because increased exportation of those products strengthens its balance of payments position. However, as other trading nations also move more and more in the direction of capital-intensive exports, Japan will have to retain the old markets and cultivate new ones for such traditional labor-intensive exports as textiles (which still are one of the Big Three earners of foreign exchange, along with steel products and ships).[10]

[10] Federation of Economic Organizations, *Economic Picture of Japan*, p. 36.

Table 34 also reveals a striking development in postwar Japan's external trade. Whereas Japan's prewar exports were almost equally divided between Asia and the rest of the importing areas, its postwar exports (especially for the 1961–63 period) were almost equally divided among Asia, the United States, and the rest of the world, indicating the greater importance of the U.S. to Japan as a customer[11] and the smaller importance of Asia and Europe. The table also implies that Japan's postwar loss of Asian markets has been somewhat compensated for by increased sales to South American and African markets. This statement, however, should be qualified by noting the increasing tendency of Japanese exporters to trade with Mainland China despite political obstacles and economic restrictions on both sides, as well as the tendency of South America and Africa not to buy from Japan for economic and geographic reasons. The smaller importance of Europe as a Japanese customer is largely the result of the European Economic Community's discriminatory tariff policy against Japanese goods in spite of Japan's membership in the General Agreement on Tariffs and Trade or perhaps because of that membership (since Western European nations have invoked Article 35 of GATT against Japan).[12] The 1968 figures indicate that the direction of Japan's exports has not changed substantially, with the possible exception of Mainland China.

As for the prospects of greater exports to the United States, Japanese exporters seem cautiously optimistic, their caution being based on America's

Table 34.   *The Changing Direction of Japan's Exports*

Destination	Export Distribution Ratio			
	1934–36	1953–55	1961–63	1968
	%	%	%	%
Asia*	52.5	46.3	34.4	28.2
Europe	10.7	9.6	16.0	12.5
U.S.	20.8	19.4	27.1	31.4
South America	2.8	7.2	7.3	5.7
Africa	7.7	9.6	8.2	5.1
Eastern bloc**	–	0.3	3.0	4.5
Mainland China	–	1.1	0.8	2.5

SOURCE: adapted from 1963 *Honbo Keizai Tokei*.
   *The figure for 1934–36 includes prewar China; those for 1953–55 and 1961–63 exclude Mainland China.
   **The figures exclude those for Mainland China, which are shown separately. The 1968 figures are from Oriental Economist, *Japan Economic Yearbook*, p. 68.

[11] See the series of publications by the United States-Japan Trade Council.
[12] Federation of Economic Organizations, *Economic Picture of Japan*, pp. 42–43. See also Japan Committee for Economic Development, "A Statement of National Policy," pp. 8–9.

high-tariff policy,[13] the instability of the American demand for Japanese consumer goods, the inherent lack of complementary trade between two nations producing competitive capital-intensive products, and the Japanese fear of excessive dependence on the American market.[14] The share of the Eastern bloc as a whole (of which the U.S.S.R. accounts for the largest component) is still quantitatively insignificant, but Japanese exporters seem hopeful of greater exports to that bloc as a possible byproduct of the general easing of East-West tensions. [15]

Let us discuss the export side further, with a view to gaining some insight into Japan's export position vis-à-vis other countries. The export ratios in Table 35 measure the different degrees to which the selected countries

Table 35. International Comparison of Export Ratios and Export and Industrial Growth Rates

Country	Export Ratio, 1961	Rate of Growth of Exports, 1953–59	Rate of Growth of Industrial Output, 1953–59
	%	%	%
Japan	8.9	19.4	12.74
West Germany	16.4	14.49	8.74
Italy	11.9	11.76	7.40
U.K.	13.7	3.66	2.55
U.S.	4.0	3.40	1.30

SOURCE: the export ratios for 1961 are based on Japanese Ministry of International Trade and Industry's 1963 White Paper on foreign commerce; the "export ratio" here refers to value of exports divided by nominal GNP. The rates of growth of exports and industrial output for 1953-59 are adapted from M. Shinohara's "Economic Development and Foreign Trade in Pre-War Japan," p. 46; the figures for both rates are those computed by Professor Shinohara from data in the United Nations Statistical Yearbook for 1959.

depend on exports as earners of foreign exchange to pay for imports, as generators of aggregate demand to help sustain aggregate supply, and as contributors to "warranted growth." This last role is most important in the present context of a growing open economy, as will be shown in the next section. Table 35 indicates that, as of 1961, Germany depended on exports most, while the U.S. depended on them least. Japan's ratio was then nearly half that of Germany and more than twice that of the U.S. Japan's low figure

[13] United States-Japan Trade Council, Protectionism in Disguise.

[14] Federation of Economic Organizations, Economic Picture of Japan, pp. 43-44.

[15] Professor S. Tsuru observes: "So long as Japan has to depend upon America, for filling her dollar gap in the balance of payments, she is likely to be all the more dependent politically on America, which fact in turn will make it more and more difficult for her to open free economic intercourse with the continent of Asia" (Essays on Japanese Economy, p. 36).

implies that exports, while important from the short-run standpoint of balance of payments equilibrium, nevertheless play a relatively smaller role in the country's rapid growth than purely domestic factors (especially private fixed investment). In view of its slow long-run growth, Britain's export ratio seems to reflect its short-run need for exports primarily as a source of aggregate demand and exchange earnings. Contrariwise, Italy's export ratio seems to reflect its long-run need for exports principally as a stimulant to rapid domestic growth.

The table also shows that exports grew at uniformly higher rates than did industrial output for all the industrial countries selected. The principal explanation for this seems to be that export markets expanded more rapidly under the impetus of global economic development and international trade liberalization than did domestic industrial markets under the distracting influence of the growing service or tertiary sector. More interesting is the existence of a strong correlation between the rates of growth of exports and the rates of growth of industrial output for the 1953–59 period. The three top-growth countries, Japan, Germany, and Italy may have achieved this status because of rapid export expansion or because of rapid industrial expansion. These two explanations apply in reverse to the low-growth countries Britain and the U.S.

Japan achieved the highest rate of growth of the selected countries in industrial production as well as in exports, and from this Professor M. Shinohara inferred that "the high export growth rate [of postwar Japan] seems to have a leading, causative role in industrial development."[16] This inference, however, remains inconclusive, not only because Japan's export expansion depends on so many external factors (foreign propensities to import, foreign price-income elasticities of demand for imports, foreign import controls, foreign import-substituting industrialization, foreign economic policies, etc.), but also because its industrial output expansion depends on so many internal factors (domestic propensities to save and to invest, domestic technological coefficients, domestic interindustry labor mobility, domestic sectoral market shares, domestic fiscal-monetary policies, etc.). In short, such a multiplicity of external and internal factors affect both exports and industrial production that it is not safe to impute a priori causality to export expansion, especially in postwar Japan with its powerful internal drive for rapid growth. On balance, I find myself inclined rather more toward the opposite view that Japan's postwar overall growth (including the rapid growth of industrial output, particularly along the lines of universally demanded products of heavy industry and consumer durables) has "a leading, causative role" in its export expansion, given the usual ceteris paribus condition.

[16] Shinohara, "Economic Development and Foreign Trade in Pre-War Japan," p. 46.

ILLUSTRATIVE MODELS OF TRADE AND GROWTH

With the foregoing analysis and interpretation of empirical data as our background, we may now turn to the consideration of some illustrative models of trade and growth that might suggest theoretically sound ways of achieving sustained growth without a chronic balance of payments deficit not only for Japan but for other trading nations as well.

Required Export Growth for External Equilibrium

The rate of foreign exchange accumulation and the rate of foreign exchange decumulation are defined, respectively, in

$$(1.1) \quad g^r(t) \equiv \frac{\Delta R_t}{R_{t-1}} = \frac{X_t - M_t}{\sum_{t=2}^{t} (X_{t-1} - M_{t-1})}$$

$$(1.2) \quad -g^r(t) \equiv \frac{\Delta R_t}{R_{t-1}} = \frac{M_t - X_t}{\sum_{t=2}^{t} (M_{t-1} - X_{t-1})}$$

Here R is the level of foreign exchange reserves, X is real exports (visible and invisible), M is real imports (visible and invisible), g^r is the positive rate of growth of exchange reserves, $-g^r$ is the negative rate of growth of exchange reserves, and t is time. Definitional equations (1.1) and (1.2) imply that a persistent export surplus causes exchange reserves to accumulate over time, while a persistent import surplus causes them to decumulate over time. The latter spells a chronic balance of payments crisis. This leads us to the necessity of determining the required rate of growth of exports relative to the given rate of growth of imports for long-run balance of payments equilibrium.

Suppose that domestic income grows according to

$$(1.3) \quad Y_d(t) = Y_d(0)(1 + g_d)^t \quad (g_d \equiv \Delta Y_d / Y_d)$$

where Y_d is the level of national output and g_d is the rate of growth of that output, $Y_d(0)$ being the initial value of the variable. Suppose, further, that a trading nation's elasticity of imports with respect to domestic income is given by

$$(1.4) \quad \epsilon = \frac{\Delta M/M}{\Delta Y_d / Y_d} \quad (\epsilon = \epsilon_t = \text{const.})$$

Taking (1.3) and (1.4) into account, we can derive the rate of growth of imports:

$$(1.5) \quad g_m \equiv \frac{\Delta M}{M} = \epsilon g_d \quad (g_m = g_m(t) = \text{const.})$$

which we shall assume to be known and given in advance. To give empirical plausibility to equation (1.5) we may substitute such numerical values for ϵ and g_d as were used by the Japanese Economic Planning Agency for the terminal planning year of 1970, namely, ϵ = 1.19 and g_d = 0.072. This entails g_m = 0.08368, or roughly 8.4 percent, as the empirically plausible rate of growth of imports in the Japanese case. As a matter of fact, the Planning Agency's 1961 *New Long-Range Economic Plan of Japan* estimates 8.4 percent to be the probable rate of growth of Japanese imports for 1970. However, in view of increasing trade liberalization all round and the recently rising propensity to import (a larger m entering $M = mY_d$, where m is the average propensity to import), it would seem advisable to be prepared for a higher rate of growth of imports than the presently estimated figure of 8.4 percent. The trend value of the elasticity of imports with respect to domestic income (ϵ) is likely to rise somewhat above the present level of 1.19, even if we make the favorable assumption that the projected rate of growth of national output can be held constant at the projected level of 7.2 percent.

Turning now to the determination of export growth, let world income as a whole grow according to

$$(1.6) \quad Y_w(t) = Y_w(0)(1 + g_w)^t \quad (g_w \equiv \Delta Y_w/Y_w)$$

where Y_w is world income and g_w is the rate of growth of world income, $Y_w(0)$ being the initial value of the variable.

Suppose that a trading nation's trend elasticity of exports with respect to world income is given by

$$(1.7) \quad \eta = \frac{\Delta X/X}{\Delta Y_w/Y_w} \quad (\eta = \eta_t = \text{const.})$$

Taking (1.6) and (1.7) into consideration, we can have the rate of growth of exports:

$$(1.8) \quad g_x \equiv \frac{\Delta X}{X} = \eta g_w \quad (g_x = g_x(t) \neq \text{const.})$$

which we shall have to adjust to any given rate of growth of imports (g_m) if chronic balance of payments difficulties are to be avoided. Here again we may substitute plausible numerical values for η and g_w. During the ten-year period 1954–64 Japan's exports grew at the average annual rate of 14.7 percent, while world income (representing world trade)[17] grew at the annual average rate of 6.8 percent, according to OECD surveys.[18] This entails 2.16 as the elasticity of Japanese exports with respect to world income. Indeed, Mr. H. Kanamori (research chief of the Japanese Economic Planning Agency) estimated the recent elasticity of Japanese exports with respect to world trade to be as high as 4 on the basis of g_w = 0.08 and g_x = 0.33 $[\eta = (g_x/g_w) \sim 4]$.[19] In view, however, of persistent U.S. balance of payments difficulties and the slow growth of output among major trading nations (especially the U.K.), it would seem safer to envisage a smaller export elasticity than Mr. Kanamori's figure. If we assign the more conservative values of 0.05 and 1.74 to g_w and η, respectively, we would come up with g_x = 0.087, or 8.7 percent according to equation (1.8). This is exactly the figure originally estimated (in 1961) by the Japanese Economic Planning Agency to be the probable rate of growth of exports for 1970, even if we do not know their specific assumptions about the secular behavior of g_w and η.

In the light of (1.3)–(1.8) the dynamic condition for the balance of trade equilibrium to be satisfied is given by

$$(1.9) \quad g_x(t) = g_m(t) \text{ or } \eta g_w(t) - \epsilon g_d(t) = 0.$$

This equilibrium condition implies the following balance of payments tendencies: if $\eta g_w(t) - \epsilon g_d(t) = 0$, then $g^r(t) = 0$ (stability of exchange reserves); if $\eta g_w(t) - \epsilon g_d(t) > 0$, then $g^r(t) > 0$ (accumulation of exchange reserves); if $\eta g_w(t) - \epsilon g_d(t) < 0$, then $g^r(t) < 0$ (decumulation of exchange reserves). Thus the actual rate of growth of exports (g_x) must be adjusted over time to any given rate of growth of imports (g_m) by reference to those trend forces which govern the secular behavior of η and g_w (both national and international forces, that is), and in such a way as to make for $g^r(t) > 0$, as the case may be.

[17] If the average world propensity to import (m) is assumed to remain constant and if world imports and world exports are in equilibrium, then world trade and world income come to be interchangeable:

$$\frac{\Delta M_w}{M_w} = \frac{m_w \Delta Y_w}{m_w Y_w} = \frac{\Delta Y_w}{Y_w} \equiv g_w \quad \left(\overline{m}_w = \frac{M_w}{Y_w} = \frac{\Delta M_w}{\Delta Y_w}, \ M_w = X_w, \ \Delta M_w = \Delta X_w \right)$$

where m_w is the world average and marginal propensity to import and $\overline{m}_w$ is the constant import ratio, while the subscript w denotes the variables in global terms.

[18] OECD, *Economic Surveys: Japan.*

[19] Kanamori, "Yagate Antei Seicho No Kodoe."

Price Elasticities and Trade Expansion

In our preceding model we tacitly assumed constant export and import prices in order to concentrate on the impact of income growth on foreign trade. We shall relax that assumption this time in order to see what difference changes in export and import prices would make to the growth of exports and imports and, by implication, to the balance of payments in an open economy like the Japanese. In static theory "worsened" terms of trade is looked upon as militating against domestic welfare, since fewer physical imports can be had per unit of exports if the average export price is lower than the average import price.[20] However, in dynamic theory it is the higher rate of decrease in the export price relative to the given rate of decrease in the import price that stimulates export expansion relative to import expansion, to the long-run benefit of balance of payments equilibrium. This is another dichotomy between static and dynamic theories.[21]

The following illustrative model will be built by abstracting from income growth and on the general simplifying assumption that exchange rates remain constant throughout the discussion. It is understood at the outset that a price elasticity of demand is generally negative (since the amount demanded is normally a decreasing function of price) but that the convention allows us to drop the minus sign.

Generally, an increase in labor productivity entails a rise in the money wage rate, a fall in the average price, and a fall in the wage-distribution ratio:

$$(2.1) \quad \rho \equiv \frac{Y}{N} = \frac{w}{\delta p} \quad \left(\delta = \frac{wN}{pY} \right)$$

where ρ is the average productivity of labor, w is the money wage rate, p is the index of general prices, and δ is the wage-distribution ratio, Y and N being national output and labor input, respectively. Equation (2.1) shows that labor productivity is positively correlated with the money wage rate and negatively correlated with general prices as well as with the wage-distribution ratio. Solving (2.1) for p yields

$$(2.2) \quad p = \frac{w/\rho}{\delta}$$

which shows that general prices, ceteris paribus, would fall with rising labor productivity and rise with falling labor productivity, given constant w and δ.

---

[20] Given $p_m M = p_x X$, we get $p_x/p_m = M/X$ (which is the familiar barter terms of trade). Here M is real imports, X is real exports, p_m is the average import price, and p_x is the average export price.

[21] Also recall the demand-decreasing role of savings in Keynes's static short-run theory vs. the resource-releasing role of savings in Harrod's dynamic long-run theory.

Equation (2.2) indicates that international price differentials can be explained basically by reference to the diverse institutional-technological complexes of nations affecting the behavior of w, ρ, and δ.

Next, let us make the simplifying assumptions

$$(2.3) \quad p_x = p_d = \left(\frac{w/\rho}{\delta}\right)_d$$

$$(2.4) \quad p_m = p_w = \left(\frac{w/\rho}{\delta}\right)_w$$

Here p_x is the average export price, p_m is the average import price, p_d is the general price index of the domestic economy, and p_w is that of the rest of the world; the subscripts d and w denote the variables in terms of the domestic and world economies. It is, in this context, best to think of domestic and world prices as being represented by wholesale prices, as they are most nearly applicable to internationally tradeable goods and services. The simplifying assumptions expressed by (2.3) and (2.4) will facilitate the subsequent analysis.

Suppose that the export price decreases according to

$$(2.5) \quad p_x(t) = p_x(0)(1 - \xi)^t \qquad (\xi \equiv \Delta p_x/p_x)$$

where ξ is the rate of decrease in the export price, $p_x(0)$ is the initial value of the variable, and t is time. Let this ξ involved in (2.5) enter the elasticity of exports with respect to price:

$$(2.6) \quad \eta_p = \frac{\Delta X/X}{\Delta p_x/p_x} \qquad (\eta_p = \eta_p(t) = \text{const.})$$

where η_p is the trend value of the export elasticity in question. It is to be noted that this export elasticity given by (2.6) represents the elasticity of world demand for imports with respect to the average import prices (export price from the national point of view).

From (2.5) and (2.6) we derive the rate of growth of exports (g_x):

$$(2.7) \quad g_x(t) \equiv \frac{\Delta X}{X} = \eta_p \xi(t)$$

which shows the possibility of exports growing at a rate equal to the price elasticity of exports (η_p) times the rate of decrease in the export price (ξ). Suppose, on the other hand, that the import price decreases according to

$$(2.8) \quad p_m(t) = p_m(0)(1 - \mu)^t \qquad (\mu \equiv \Delta p_m/p_m)$$

where μ is the rate of decrease in the import price, $p_m(0)$ being the initial value of the variable. Let this μ enter the price elasticity of imports:

$$(2.9) \quad \epsilon_p = \frac{\Delta M/M}{\Delta p_m/p_m} \quad [\epsilon_p = \epsilon_p(t) = \text{const.}]$$

where ϵ_p is the trend value of the price elasticity of imports. It is well to bear in mind that the average price (p_m) is set by the rest of the world.

From (2.8) and (2.9) we obtain the rate of growth of imports (g_m):

$$(2.10) \quad g_m(t) \equiv \frac{\Delta M}{M} = \epsilon_p \mu(t)$$

which indicates the possibility of imports expanding at a rate equal to the price elasticity of imports (ϵ_p) times the rate of decrease in the import price (μ).

Taking (2.5)–(2.10) into account, we may put down the condition for the balance of trade equilibrium in the form

$$(2.11) \quad g_x(t) = g_m(t) \text{ or } \eta_p \xi(t) - \epsilon_p \mu(t) = 0$$

We may generalize the implications of equation (2.11) for balance of payments equilibrium or disequilibrium, as follows: if $\eta_p = \epsilon_p$, $\xi > \mu$, then $g_x > g_m$, $g^r > 0$ (accumulation of exchange reserves); if $\eta_p > \epsilon_p$, $\xi = \mu$, then $g_x > g_m$, $g^r > 0$ (accumulation of exchange reserves); if $\eta_p < \epsilon_p$, $\xi = \mu$, then $g_x < g_m$, $g^r < 0$ (decumulation of exchange reserves); if $\eta_p = \epsilon_p$, $\xi < \mu$, then $g_x < g_m$, $g^r < 0$ (decumulation of exchange reserves). Here g^r is the rate of growth of foreign exchange reserves, as in the previous model. Of the above cases, the first and second would appeal to the Japanese economy or, for that matter, to any advanced open economy with perennial balance of payments difficulties. The first case shows that if the price elasticities of exports and imports are equal, a higher rate of decrease in the export price than in the import price will, ceteris paribus, entail greater expansion of exports than of imports and hence accumulation of exchange reserves, while the second case indicates that if the rates of decrease in the export and import prices are the same, a higher price elasticity of exports than of imports will, ceteris paribus, also give rise to a greater expansion of exports than of imports and hence the accumulation of exchange reserves.

The second case is more complex, since it involves the institutionally difficult task of making foreign customers more price-sensitive or domestic buyers of imports less price-sensitive, or both. By contrast, the former case involves the technologically feasible task of increasing productivity fast enough to lower the export price relative to any given fall in the import price, as the Japanese economy has demonstrated in recent years. However, increasing "quality competition" in the international as well as national field could conceivably counterbalance the advantage of price competition somewhat. We need not belabor the third and fourth cases, since few trading nations are interested in seeing their exchange reserves depleted for price or any other deficit-making reasons. They are added here merely for the sake of formal completeness. I leave it to econometricians to test these generalizations empirically.

The Role of the Foreign Balance in Domestic Economic Growth

Allusion was made earlier to the theoretical possibility that the foreign balance might make a direct contribution to "warranted growth," which is Sir Roy Harrod's rather familiar pattern of steady output and capital expansion with dynamic equality of investment and savings ratios at every instant of time and hence without excess or short capacity. Whether the foreign balance will or will not contribute to the realization and maintenance of such an ideal pattern of steady domestic growth depends on the trend values of the savings and capital-output ratios involved.

Let the open economy's "investment-savings" equilibrium condition take the simple form (omitting the time subscript)

$$(3.1) \quad I + X = S + M$$

where I is net investment, X is real exports (visible and invisible), S is domestic savings, and M is real imports (visible and invisible). The righthand side of the equation represents the open economy's supply of resources, while its lefthand side represents its demand for resources. All the variables of equation (3.1) can be made the dependent ones:

$$(3.2) \quad I = b\Delta Y \quad (b \equiv I/\Delta Y \equiv \Delta K/\Delta Y = \text{const.})$$
$$(3.3) \quad X = \overline{X} \quad (\overline{X}/Y \equiv x = \text{const.})$$
$$(3.4) \quad S = sY \quad (s \equiv S/Y = \text{const.})$$
$$(3.5) \quad M = mY \quad (m \equiv M/Y = \text{const.})$$

Here Y is national output, $\overline{X}$ is autonomous exports, K is real capital, b is the capital coefficient, s is the average savings ratio, and m is the average import ratio. In the light of (3.2)–(3.5), equation (3.1) can be rewritten as

$$(3.6) \quad b\Delta Y = sY + mY = xY = (s + m - x)Y$$

dividing which through by bY yields the rate of growth of output (or capital):

$$(3.7) \quad g_w \equiv \frac{\Delta Y}{Y} = \frac{s + m - x}{b}$$

This g_w given by (3.7) is what Sir Roy Harrod calls the "warranted" rate of growth for an open economy. It includes the possible influence of the foreign balance expressed in $m - x$. The respective contributions of the export and import ratios to the open economy's "investment-savings" equilibrium can be seen more clearly by transposing (3.7):

$$(3.8) \quad bg_w + x = s + m; \quad \left(\frac{I}{\Delta Y}\right)\left(\frac{\Delta Y}{Y}\right) = \frac{I}{Y} = \frac{S}{Y} + \frac{M}{Y} - \frac{X}{Y}$$

which reveals that the export ratio (x) contributes to the demand-for-resources side (left), while the import ratio (m) contributes to the supply-of-resources side (right) in an open economy growing at the "warranted" rate g_w. Such contributions to "warranted" growth provide the analytical significance of the export and import ratios discussed earlier in some detail). Furthermore, the export and import ratios regarded as independent variables in equation (3.7) have practical implications for the open economy's balance of payments position on capital account. An import surplus (expressible in $m - x > 0$) implies net foreign borrowing in most instances (unless it can be financed out of gold and exchange reserves without resorting to long-term capital imports). Conversely, an export surplus (expressible in $m - x < 0$) implies net foreign lending.

We may contemplate various possible foreign balance positions associated with different savings and capital-output ratios, according to equation (3.7). Table 36 provides a numerical model for this purpose. The table indicates that an open economy with a high savings ratio and a low capital-output ratio

Table 36. The Hypothetical Foreign Balance and Domestic Growth

Foreign Balance Position	Savings Ratio	Import Ratio	Export Ratio	Capital-Output Ratio	Given Growth Rate
$(s + m - x)/b = \bar{g}$					
Trade balance $(m - x = 0)$	.25	.10	.10	2.5	.10
Import surplus $(m - x > 0)$	.20	.20	.10	3.0	.10
Export surplus $(m - x < 0)$	.15	.10	.15	1.0	.10

need not depend so much on the foreign balance for achieving a given target rate of growth of national output. The figures for all the variables in Table 36 are empirically plausible in view of our previous international comparison of those variables. The first foreign balance position seems to be what the Japanese economy has been trying to achieve and maintain, while the last position seems to be what it would like to achieve and maintain in the 1970s (though it aims at a much more modest target rate of growth than shown in the table, i.e., 7.2 percent). That is to say, if the savings ratio falls to a lower level while productivity of capital rises to a much higher level (as implied by the low capital-output ratio of 1 involved in the third position), then the Japanese economy will be able to enjoy a persistent export surplus in terms of ratios as well as a high rate of growth of national output. Meanwhile, the Japanese economy may find itself lingering in the second position, endeavoring to maintain its high rate of growth of output with a minimal deficit in capital transactions [implicit in $(m - x > 0)$].

APPENDIX: OBSERVATIONS ON JAPAN'S TEN-YEAR GROWTH PLAN

Japan achieved an average annual GNP growth rate of 8.5 percent for the postwar period 1950-57, as compared with Germany's 8 percent, Russia's 6 percent, and the U.S.'s 4 percent for the same period.[1] However, little is known outside Japan about her income-doubling plan for the coming decade. This plan is based on the Japanese government's *New Long-Range Economic Plan of Japan, 1961-70* and its Economic White Paper (*Keizai Hakusho*).[2] Even less is known about a more ambitious growth plan called the Shimomura model, which was prepared by Dr. Osamu Shimomura of the government-owned development bank (Nippon Kaihatsu Ginko).[3] The Japanese Economic Planning Agency's Economic White Paper cautiously envisages an annual GNP growth rate of around 7.2 percent as plausible for the coming decade in Japan, whereas the Shimomura model optimistically predicts a growth rate of 10 percent or more as an achievable and sustainable figure.

These specific projections have been criticized on various grounds by Japanese economists themselves,[4] but the critics have confined themselves mainly to methodological debates on statistical measurement, parameter estimation, and price deflators. I should like to make more substantive observations on Japan's ten-year growth plan, with a view to shedding light on the

---

A slightly different version of this Appendix appeared in *Kyklos*, 15 (1962).

[1] These figures are derived from Governor Rockefeller's *Accelerated Economic Growth—A Key to the American Future.*

[2] Japanese Economic Planning Agency, *New Long-Range Economic Plan of Japan* and *Keizai Hakusho.*

[3] The Shimomura model was first reported at the joint meeting of the Japanese Economic Association and the Japanese Econometric Society in 1960; it was subsequently published under the title "Seicho Seisaku No Kihon Mondai" [Basic problems of growth policy] in *Riron Keizaigaku*, March 1961.

[4] See S. Tsuru, "Growth and Stability in the Postwar Japanese Economy," *American Economic Review*, May 1961; Y. Shionoya, K. Baba, and M. Shinohara, "Comments on the Shimomura Model," *Riron Keizaigaku*, March 1961; M. Kushida, *Nihon Keizai No Seichoryoku* [The growth capacity of the Japanese economy] (Tokyo, 1959).

131

general possibility and difficulty of planning rapid and stable growth within the framework of a market economy. These observations will be made under five specific headings: basic differences from other national plans, the equilibrium growth of a market economy, technical innovations and growth potential, the investment-consumption relation, and public policy and growth.

BASIC DIFFERENCES FROM OTHER NATIONAL PLANS

Japan's growth plan, including both the Japanese Economic Planning Agency's income-doubling plan and the Shimomura model, differs fundamentally from its counterparts abroad in several respects. First, unlike the American economy, with no governmental growth plan,[5] the Japanese economy does have a plan prepared by a government agency in collaboration with the representatives of the private sector.[6] Second, unlike its Russian counterpart,[7] the Japanese growth plan is carried out largely by private business enterprise under the paternalistic guidance of government[8] rather than by public agencies under a central coordinating body. Last, unlike the Dutch plan[9] but like the Indian,[10] the Japanese growth plan stresses the growth potential of productive capacity more than that of effective demand.[11] These basic differences are also important for the light they throw

[5] In the United States such private agencies as the National Planning Association and the Committee for Economic Development publish long-range projections to guide and stimulate microeconomic planning on a "do it yourself" basis; see, in this respect, G. Colm and M. Young, *The Economy of the American People: Progress, Problems, Prospects* (Washington, D.C., 1962); Rockefeller, *Accelerated Economic Growth*; and A. H. Hansen, "We Must Grow—Or We Sink," *New York Times Magazine*, March 18, 1962.

[6] In Japan, there exists a public planning body known as the Economic Deliberation Council composed of industrial, financial, and professional specialists who are appointed by the Prime Minister. The economic White Papers of the Japanese Planning Agency reflect the collective wisdom of those specialists; they are implemented through the deliberate fiscal, monetary, and other policies of the government agencies having to do with private investment and other economic activities affecting the nation's economic growth and stability.

[7] See E. D. Domar, "A Soviet Model of Growth," in his *Essays in the Theory of Economic Growth* (New York, 1959); M. Dobb, *An Essay on Economic Growth and Planning* (New York, 1969); C. Bettelheim, *Studies in the Theory of Planning* (New York, 1968); and F. D. Holzman, *Readings on the Soviet Economy* (Chicago, 1961).

[8] Government paternalism will be detailed under the heading "public policy and growth" later.

[9] Central Planning Bureau (Netherlands Government), *The Scope and Methods of the Central Planning Bureau*, 1956; J. Tinbergen, *Economic Policy: Principles and Design*, 1956; and H. Thiel, *Economic Forecasts and Policy* (New York, 1961).

[10] India Planning Commission, Second Five-Year Plan, 1956; C. N. Vakil and P. R. Brahamanda, *Planning for an Expanding Economy: Accumulation, Employment and Technical Progress in Under-developed Countries*, 1956; P. C. Mahalanobis, "The Approach of Operational Research to Planning in India," *Sankhya*, December 1955; and G. P. Khare, *Planning in India*, 1958.

[11] The wisdom or unwisdom of this national idiosyncrasy will be probed in connection with the next topic.

upon the historical, institutional, political, and ideological "determinants of determinants" of the pattern as well as the speed of growth in a specific economy. The full relevance of these differences to Japan's growth potential will be explored below.

THE EQUILIBRIUM GROWTH OF A MARKET ECONOMY

Professor Tsuru's qualification about the increasing importance of the "demand situation" seems well worth heeding and exploring.[12] The Shimomura model takes the conditions of demand as given and concentrates on the supply side, as though the Japanese economy were so completely planned as to equate its demand and supply sides as a matter of course. To be sure, because of the shortage of capital (especially durable plant and equipment) during the postwar period the Japanese economy temporarily and understandably behaved like an underdeveloped economy needing greater productive capacity, rather than effective demand, but that abnormal period is over, and is once again confronted with the common problem of all advanced market economies, namely: that of equilibrating effective demand and productive capacity for equilibrium growth.[13] In this respect, the Japanese

[12] "Growth and Stability in the Postwar Japanese Economy." Professor Tsuru offers this as a qualification to "the feasibility of continuing a fairly high rate of growth in the coming decade," but he does not himself elaborate thereon.

[13] We may build an illustrative model of equilibrium growth, thus: let the multiplier expansion of effective demand take the form

$$(1.1) \quad \Delta Y_d = \frac{1}{s + t + m}(\Delta \bar{I} + \Delta \bar{G} + \Delta \bar{X}) \quad (s, t, m \neq \text{const.})$$

where Y_d is real national income demanded or simply effective demand, $\bar{I}$ is private autonomous net investment, $\bar{G}$ is autonomous government expenditure, $\bar{I}$ is private autonomous net investment, $\bar{G}$ is autonomous government expenditure, $\bar{X}$ is autonomous exports, s is the domestic marginal propensity to save, t is the government's marginal propensity to tax in general, and m is the domestic marginal propensity to import.

Putting $\Delta I/Y_d = a$, $\Delta\bar{G}/Y_d = g$, and $\Delta\bar{X}/Y_d = e$ and dividing (1.1) through by Y_d yields the rate of growth of effective demand (G_d):

$$(1.2) \quad G_d \equiv \left(\frac{\Delta Y}{Y}\right)_d = \frac{a + g + e}{s + t + m} \quad (a, g, e \neq \text{const.})$$

which represents the demand side of a growing market economy.

On the other hand, let the limiting production function of the growing economy take the form

$$(1.3) \quad \Delta Y_s = \sigma(\Delta K_p + \Delta K_g + \Delta K_m) \quad (\sigma = \text{const.})$$

where Y_s is real national income supplied by fully utilizing the existing stock of capital, K_p is private real capital, K_g is government real capital, K_m is imported real capital, and σ is the marginal and average productivity of capital for the whole economy.

Putting $\Delta K_p/Y_s = \pi$, $\Delta K_g/Y_s = \gamma$, and $\Delta K_m/Y_s = \mu$ and dividing (1.3) through by Y_s yields the rate of growth of productive capacity (G_s):

Economic Planning Agency's White Paper shows a keener awareness of the demand or expenditure side than the Shimomura model.

As Professor H. Aoyama has recently pointed out, the structural instability of the Japanese economy is still caused partly by the preponderance of cycle-sensitive export industries and partly by the precarious existence of medium and small-scale industries.[14] He implies that unless those cycle-insensitive industries which are related to government activity, population growth and technological progress (e.g., the communications, transportation, engineering, chemical, electrical, and printing industries) grow faster in the future than in the past, steady growth of net capital formation despite periodic slumps will not take place in Japan. It is by no means obvious that the Shimomura model or the Japanese Economic Planning Agency's ten-year plan can safely assume, as they seem to do, that the cycle-insensitive industries will outstrip cycle-sensitive industries in the decade ahead, especially when the latter depend so heavily on the behavior of unpredictable and uncontrollable foreign markets.[15]

TECHNOLOGICAL INNOVATIONS AND GROWTH POTENTIAL

Both the Shimomura model and the Japanese Economic Planning Agency's ten-year plan seem to underestimate the role of technological innovation in Japan's future economic growth. It is interesting that Dr. Shimomura, while recognizing an exceptionally high productivity of capital as a realistic

---

$$(1.4) \quad G_s \equiv \left(\frac{\Delta Y}{Y}\right)_s = \sigma(\pi + \gamma + \mu) \quad (\pi, \gamma, \mu = \text{const.})$$

which represents the supply side of the growing economy in question.

Then the economy must satisfy

$$(1.5) \quad \frac{a + g + e}{s + t + m} = \sigma(\pi + \gamma + \mu); \quad G_d = G_s$$

for equilibrium growth with a positive constant rate, that is, without inflationary or deflationary divergences over the entire planning horizon. But there is no reason to suppose that in mainly laissez-faire conditions the equilibrium condition specified by (1.5) will always be satisfied except by accident. Thus we may generalize what would happen if (1.5) were or were not satisfied by design (especially by operating with the variables on the lefthand side, $a, g, e, s, t,$ and m in relation to one another, as well as in a manner that would not entail an offsetting or destabilizing effect on $\pi, \gamma,$ or μ on the supply side), as follows: if $G_d < G_s$, then $dG_s/dt < 0$ for lack of demand (the case of advanced economies); if $G_d > G_s$, then $dG_d/dt < 0$ for lack of capacity (the case of underdeveloped economies); if $G_d = G_s$, then $dG/dt = dG_s/dt = 0$ (general case of equilibrium growth).

[14] Aoyama, ed., *Nihon Keizai To Keiki Hendo* (esp. chap. 1).

[15] For the uncertain dependence of Japan's economic growth on export trade see M. Shinohara, "An International Comparison of Export Expansion and Output Effects," *Riron Keizaigaku*, September 1961.

prospect in Japan, nevertheless dismisses it as causally insignificant.[16] He does this by postulating the stability of capital productivity over the projected period as well as by overlooking the demand aspect of technological progress. By contrast, Messrs. N. Noda, Y. Masuda, S. Yamazaki, and T. Nomura of the Japanese Productivity Research Center (Nihon Seisansei Honbu) have emphasized the crucial role of automation and nuclear technology in Japan's future economic growth as well as in postwar recovery and reconstruction.[17] If the trend value of capital productivity is rising, contrary to Dr. Shimomura's constancy assumption, then the same target rate of growth can be achieved with a smaller investment ratio than he deems necessary.[18] This in turn implies the possibility of rapid economic growth with an increase in domestic consumption and a decrease in imported capital in terms of ratios, as equation (1.4) of our model would indicate.

Moreover, technological innovations are capable of affecting the demand side of a growing economy, though not without some destabilizing repercussions on equilibrium growth. Modernization of plant and equipment, stressed alike by the Japanese government and the private sector, entails

[16] Shimomura, "Seicho Seisaku No Kihon Mondai." My objection to Dr. Shimomura's model, in this respect, is directed at his constancy assumption, not at his projected high productivity coefficient, which he undoubtedly estimated by taking Japan's technological progress into account.

[17] *Gijitsu To Nihon Keizai* [Technology and the Japanese economy], 1960. In this connection, it seems noteworthy that the Nippon Management Association (Nippon Noritisu Kyokai), which is a non-profit private organization devoted to the promotion of management science and technology, actively promotes the "voluntary rationalization of management" stressed by the Japanese Economic Planning Agency's White Paper.

[18] The productivity of capital (σ) is a function of labor productivity (Y/N) and the capital-labor ratio (K/N):

$$\sigma = \frac{Y}{K} = \frac{Y/N}{K/N}$$

If we assume that the automation drive increases labor productivity, we can have the exponential function of the form

$$\frac{Y}{N} = \rho_t = \rho_0(1 + \nu)^t$$

where ν is the constant rate of increase of labor productivity and ρ_0 is the initial value of that productivity. Assuming further that the capital-labor ratio is an invariant function of time ($K/N = \theta_t = $ const.), we may rewrite equation (1.4) as

$$G_s(t) = \frac{\rho_0(1 + \nu)^t}{\bar{\theta}} (\bar{\pi} + \bar{\gamma} + \bar{\mu}),$$

which clearly shows the possibility that the rate of growth of productive capacity (G_s) may increase over time as a result of labor productivity rising at the rate ν, even though the capital-labor and other ratios remain unchanged ($\theta, \pi, \gamma, \mu = $ const.).

greater and greater "innovational investment" of an autonomous nature. In terms of our model, this means that the ratio of additional private net investment to income (a) is likely to rise secularly because of a larger $\Delta \bar{I}$ relative to any Y_d, that the ratio of additional exports to income (e) is also likely to rise because of the decreasing effect of modernization on export prices, and that the marginal propensity to import (m) is likely to be reduced by the import-substituting industrialization which technological progress makes possible. As a consequence of all this, Japan's rate of growth of effective demand (G_d) may well increase sufficiently to support the target rate of growth of productive capacity (G_s), as equations (1.1) and (1.2) of footnote 13 would predict. Thus, if the favorable effects of technological progress on the demand as well as the supply side are taken into account, Japan's growth potential may be as great as the Shimomura model, albeit without attaching much significance to the technological factor, optimistically envisages. A series of such technological impacts, in addition, could conceivably offset all the bottlenecks implied in Professor Tsuru's qualifications,[19] though one might not wish to go as far as Schumpeter's monistic theory of innovation.[20]

THE INVESTMENT-CONSUMPTION RELATION

In a significant footnote Dr. Shimomura reveals a key to Japan's high-saving, high-investment dynamics.[21] He urges a financial policy dynamic enough to enable Japan to liberate itself from the traditional static concept of savings-investment equilibrium, though he fails to demonstrate a functional relation between such a financial policy and the amazingly high target investment ratio of nearly 30 percent envisaged in his growth model.[22] The

[19] "Growth and Stability in the Postwar Japanese Economy." In addition to the increasing importance of the "demand situation" already mentioned, Professor Tsuru alludes to the greater and perhaps more taxing requirement of export expansion to secure requisite raw materials, the growing share of immediately unproductive public investment in the nation's limited capital resources, and the crucial yet difficult problem of labor immobility as an institutional impediment to economic growth.

[20] J. A. Schumpeter, *The Theory of Economic Development* (Cambridge, Mass., 1934). The aforementioned authors of *Gijitsu To Nihon Keizai* seem to have carried Schumpeter's theory a little too far, overlooking the danger of instability arising from the interdependent effects of innovation on the demand and the supply sides of a growing economy.

[21] Shimomura, "Seicho Seisaku No Kihon Mondai."

[22] We may approximate the operational possibility of the Shimomura model thus: let the credit-creating Japanese economy have the following structural parametric values:

(2.1) $I/\Delta Y = b = 2.5$

$S/Y = s = 0.15$

$D/Y = d = 0.1$

where Y is real national income or output, S is private savings, I is private net investment in fixed capital, D is autonomous long-term credit supplied by the banking system (including Shimo-

"liberation" he deems necessary seems to be a reference to the classical assumption that greater investment must inevitably necessitate greater saving at the expense of consumption. However, Dr. Shimomura tacitly accepts Sir Dennis Robertson's neoclassical savings-investment theory that today's demand for investible funds can exceed today's supply of savings out of yesterday's income by an amount equal to "dishoarding,"[23] though Dr. Shimomura presumably would substitute public long-term credit for the private savers' dishoarding. Professor Tsuru alludes to such long-term credit when he mentions the Japanese government's "gigantic industry-financing program . . . aimed at specific industries and investment programs."[24]

In the light of such financial arrangements in Japan, it is not surprising that Dr. Shimomura should make a seemingly paradoxical reference to Japan's "rate of [capital] accumulation remaining very high despite her rising consumption level."[25] If, therefore, greater investment can be financed partly

---

mura's Development Bank and the Long-Term Credit Bank of Japan, in the present context), b is the capital-output ratio (since $I \equiv \Delta K$), s is the savings ratio, and d is the ratio of autonomous credit to national income considered as a fixed desideratum (and datum). The corresponding parametric values are not implausible if judged by the Japanese literature which has been cited (see, in addition, Bank of Japan Economic Research Department, *Flow of Funds in the Japanese Economy during 1959* [Tokyo, 1960]). In the light of (2.1) we may equate the economy's aggregate induced investment to its aggregate "saving" in the form

(2.2) $b\Delta Y = sY + dY = (s + d)Y$

dividing which through by Y and rearranging gives a 10 percent rate of growth (G):

(2.3) $G \equiv \dfrac{\Delta Y}{Y} = \dfrac{s + d}{b} = \dfrac{0.15 + 0.1}{2.5} = 0.1$

Equation (2.3) implies a 25 percent investment ratio, since

(2.4) $b\dfrac{\Delta Y}{Y} = \left(\dfrac{I}{Y}\right)\left(\dfrac{\Delta Y}{Y}\right) = \dfrac{I}{Y}$ or $2.5 \times 0.1 = 0.25$

The investment ratio given by (2.4) is what must be equated to the credit-creating economy's total "saving" including long-term credit:

(2.5) $\dfrac{I}{Y} = \dfrac{S}{Y} + \dfrac{\overline{D}}{Y}$ or $bG = s + d;\ 0.25 = 0.15 + 0.1$

which is the condition for what Sir Roy Harrod calls "progressive equilibrium," albeit in an explicitly credit-creating setting (see his *Towards a Dynamic Economics*).

[23] D. H. Robertson, "Saving and Hoarding," *Economic Journal*, September 1933. Robertson's notion that savings plus "dishoarding" represent potential investible funds is essentially the same as Schumpeter's idea of "credit" as constituting an explanatory variable of economic development on a par with "innovation" and "entrepreneurship."

[24] Tsuru, "Growth and Stability in the Postwar Japanese Economy."

[25] Shimomura, "Seicho Seisaku No Kihon Mondai."

by credits, there is no need for that "abstinence" which the classical economists considered necessary for economic progress, any more than there is for that "austerity" which some present-day underdeveloped economies attempt to impose on already underconsuming populations at the constant peril of social unrest. Nor is it difficult, in such credit-creating circumstances, to agree with Keynes that consumption and investment should be considered complementary rather than competitive. [26]

PUBLIC POLICY AND GROWTH

The Shimomura model limits the government role largely to a bolder monetary-fiscal policy of sustaining a high level of aggregate demand without the orthodox fear of inflation. It deems such a public policy essential to the rapid growth of productive capacity in Japan, while at the same time the star role is assigned to the private inducement to invest in plant and equipment. The Japanese Economic Planning Agency shows a greater concern for public investment, though apparently considering it an additional claim on the country's limited savings potential rather than as a pump-primer of demand. In the same way, Professor Tsuru refers to Japan's "social overhead structure" as requiring "a greater share of the total capital needs in the future"—as if to nullify his own acknowledgment of the government's "gigantic industry-financing program."[27] Professor Tsuru's concern seems unconvincing, inasmuch as he does not explore the far-reaching significance of his passing allusion to public investment as "providing external economies for the private sector." In addition to possessing its own intrinsic merits, public investment in transportation and communications facilities, public education, health, and welfare projects, and other external economies is capable of increasing general productivity and hence the overall growth rate through its decreasing effect on the capital-output ratio (or, what is the same, through its increasing effect on capital productivity). [28]

Accordingly, the government's "social investment" is not, as the Japanese Economic Planning Agency and Professor Tsuru seem to fear, a limiting factor in Japan's future economic growth, especially if one takes a longer view than a ten-year planning horizon would permit. In this respect, what Professor Galbraith recommends to underdeveloped economies seems applicable even to advanced economies, including that of Japan.[29] Moreover,

[26]"Capital is not a self-subsistent entity existing apart from consumption. On the contrary, every weakening in the propensity to consume regarded as a permanent habit must weaken the demand for capital as well as the demand for consumption" (*General Theory of Employment, Interest, and Money*, p. 106).

[27]Tsuru, "Growth and Stability in the Postwar Japanese Economy."

[28]The reader is referred to footnote 18 above.

[29]"Education and Economic Development: An Economist's View," *Kautilya* (published by Mysore University, India), January 1962.

unless Japan's public investment were wholly of the pyramid-building variety, it would contribute directly to her growth of productive capacity, as I have elsewhere indicated[30] in discussing an economy lacking a strong private propensity to invest yet possessing a parliamentary will to let the state assume "an ever greater responsibility for directly organizing investment" and "on long views and on the basis of the general social advantage" in a Keynesian manner.[31] Be that as it may, it seems rash to conclude, as some outside observers seem inclined to do, that Japan's spectacular growth performance is prima facie evidence of a market economy's innate ability to outstrip a planned economy under any circumstances. Anyone acquainted with Japan's deepseated tradition of governmental paternalism, with all its delicate and intricate implications, would seriously doubt that, without a vigorous and conscious public policy to guide and implement private initiative, the Japanese economy could have achieved or would be able to sustain a rate of growth as high as that contemplated by the Japanese Economic Planning Agency or the Shimomura model.

CONCLUDING REMARKS

Given such democratic welfare state objectives[32] as social insurance, full employment, smaller income-wealth disparities, and higher consumption standards (avowed Japanese goals, according to the government's Economic White Paper), a mere projection or mechanical extrapolation of past trends must be replaced by imaginative yet rigorous programming techniques for optimal growth with a clear-cut target function as well as explicit constraints (e.g., minimum reducible consumption, minimum unemployment, maximum deficits, and maximum consumer price stability). In this regard, what Professors J. Tinbergen and S. Ichimura have done for underdeveloped economies seems promising and challenging even from the standpoint of advanced economies, including the Japanese.[33] Further, given such scarce resources as are associated with the Japanese and British economies,[34] a market economy's "planning" would probably have to go somewhat beyond conventional fiscal-monetary policies for stability and growth, though without sacri-

[30] "The Fiscal Role of Government in Economic Development," *Indian Journal of Economics*, July 1956.

[31] *General Theory of Employment, Interest, and Money*, p. 164.

[32] For a penetrating essay on this subject see G. Myrdal, *Beyond the Welfare State: Economic Planning in the Welfare States and Its International Implications* (New Haven, Conn., 1960).

[33] See mathematical appendixes in United Nations, *Programming Techniques for Economic Development* (New York, 1960), with special reference to Asia and the Far East).

[34] Professor T. Barna's keen appreciation of the need for a full-employment public policy and other welfare state measures as requisites for private confidence and expansion in the British economy seems highly relevant to the Japanese economy, with as few resources but without as many welfare state commitments. See his *Investment and Growth Policies in British Industrial Firms*.

ficing essential liberties. This might mean a new combination of a more direct public campaign to promote technological progress instead of relying exclusively on "voluntary rationalization of management," a more comprehensive public policy to coordinate individual investment decisions as well as regional public investment programs, and a more concerted attempt to stabilize those structurally cycle-sensitive private industries which would otherwise weaken a market economy's growth potential. Finally, given the competitive growth drives of the completely planned economies and the new underdeveloped economies which are challenging the advanced market economies, Japan will find it necessary to pay far greater attention to the productivity aspect of the "demonstration effect" than to its consumption aspect in an understandable effort to keep up with the international Joneses or to keep ahead of the international Smiths. The implication is that the Japanese economy would do well to replace its strong proclivity to emulate the high consumption standards of the U.S. and European economies with an even stronger imitation of the superior technology and productivity of those economies.

The foregoing observations may serve as a useful addition to the international growth policy debate in general and the Japanese growth controversy in particular. They may also suggest further ways to apply modern dynamic economics with due regard to existing national peculiarities and changing international circumstances.

SELECTED BIBLIOGRAPHY

Abe, G., "Competition and Monopoly in the Japanese Economy." In *Wirtschaftssysteme Des Westens: Economic Systems of the West*, edited by R. Frei. Basel, 1957–59.

Allen, G. C. "Factors in Japan's Economic Growth." In *The Economic Development of China and Japan*, edited by C. D. Cowan. London, 1964.

———. *Japan's Economic Expansion*. London, 1965.

Aoyama, H., *Nihon Keizai To Keiki Hendo* [The Japanese economy and the trade cycle]. Tokyo, 1957.

Bronfenbrenner, M. "Economic Miracles and Japan's Income-Doubling Plan." In *The State and Economic Enterprise in Japan*, edited by W. W. Lockwood. Princeton, N.J., 1965.

———. "Formalizing the Shimomura Growth Model." *Economic Development and Cultural Change*. October 1965.

———. " 'Excessive Competition' in Japanese Business." *Monumenta Nipponica* (Sophia University, Tokyo). Vol. 21 (1966).

Bronfenbrenner, M., and Kogiku, K. "The Aftermath of the Shoup Tax Reforms." *National Tax Journal*. September and December 1957.

Committee for Economic Development. *Japan in the Free World Economy*. New York, 1963.

Cowan, C. D., ed. *The Economic Development of China and Japan*. London, 1964.

Dore, R. P. "Watakushi No Nihon Keizairon: Nihon Keizaihatten No Shakaiteki Haikei" [My theory of the Japanese economy: The social background of Japanese economic growth]. *Japan Economic Research Center Monthly Report*. September 1965.

Economist (London). "Year of the Open Door: The Economist Reconsiders Japan" (special issue on Japan). November 28, 1964.

Eguchi, T. Keizai Seicho To Tsuika Shinyo" [Economic growth and ancillary credit]. *Keizai Orai* [Economic Comings and Goings]. June 1966.

Emi, K. *Government Fiscal Activity and Economic Growth in Japan, 1868–1960*. Tokyo, 1963.

Federation of Economic Organizations [Keidanren]. *Economic Picture of Japan.* Tokyo, 1964.
_____. *Japan Striving for Better Global Co-operation.* Tokyo, 1965.
Fujioka, M. "Japan's Plan to Double Income." *Fund and Bank Review.* June 1964.
Hayashi, Y. "Capital Accumulation and Taxation in Japan," *National Tax Journal,* June 1963.
Hayashi, Y., and Shima, Y., eds. *Zaisei Seisaku No Riron* [Theory of fiscal policy]. Tokyo, 1964.
Ichimura, S. *Nihon Keizai No Kozo* [The structure of the Japanese economy]. Tokyo, 1957.
_____. *Sekai No Nakano Nihon Keizai* [The Japanese economy in the world]. Tokyo, 1965.
Iida, K. *Keizai Seicho To Nijyu Kozo* [Economic growth and the dual structure]. Tokyo, 1962.
Iochi, R. *Measurement of Consumer Price Changes by Income Classes.* Tokyo, 1964.
Iwanami symposium. *See* Ohuchi, H., et al.
Japan Committee for Economic Development [Keizai Doyukai]. "Japan in the World Economy." In *Japan in the Free World Economy.* New York, 1963.
Japan Economic Research Center [Nihon Keizai Kenjyu Senta]. "Tokushu: Keizai Hakusho" [Special issue on the Economic White Paper]. *Japan Economic Research Center Monthly Report.* September 1965.
Japanese Economic Planning Agency. *Nihon Keizai No Choki Tenbo* [A long-run view of the Japanese economy]. Tokyo, 1960.
_____. *Sengo Nihon No Keizai Seicho* [The economic growth of postwar Japan]. Tokyo, 1960.
_____. *New Long-Range Economic Plan of Japan, 1961-1970.* Tokyo, 1961.
_____. *Keizai Hakusho: Kokumin Seikatsu* [White Paper on national living]. Tokyo, 1962.
_____. *Keizai Hakusho: Antei Seicho No Kadai* [White Paper on stable growth]. Tokyo, 1965.
Japan Management Association [Nippon Noritsu Kyokai]. *Gijitsu To Nihon Keizai* [Technology and the Japanese economy]. Tokyo, 1962.
Kamakura, N. *Nihon Keizairon* [A theory of the Japanese economy]. Tokyo, 1965.
Kanamori, H. *Nihon No Boeki* [Japan's foreign trade]. Tokyo, 1961.
Klein, L. R. "A Model of Japanese Economic Growth, 1878-1937." *Econometrica.* July 1961.
Klein, L. R., and Shinkai, Y. "An Econometric Model of Japan, 1930-1959." *International Economic Review.* January 1963.

Kodera, T. "Post-War Inflation in Japan." *Kwansei Gakuin University Annual Studies*. August 1953.

Kojima, K., ed. *Ronso: Keizai Seicho To Nihon Boeki* [Debate: economic growth and Japanese foreign trade]. Tokyo, 1960.

Komiya, R., ed. *Sengo Nihon No Keizai Seicho* [Postwar Japan's Economic Growth] (English translation available). Tokyo, 1964.

Kurihara, K. K. "Post-War Inflation and Fiscal-Monetary Policy of Japan." *American Economic Review*, December 1946.

_____. "Japan's Trade Position in a Changing World Market." *Review of Economics and Statistics*. November 1955.

_____. "Observations on Japan's Ten-Year Growth Plan." *Kyklos*. Vol. 15 (1962). (Appendix to this volume.)

Lockwood, W. W., ed. *The State and Economic Enterprise in Japan*. Princeton, N.J., 1965.

Nakayama, I., ed. *Nihon Keizai No Seicho* [The growth of the Japanese economy]. Tokyo, 1960.

Ohkawa, K. *The Growth Rate of the Japanese Economy since 1878*. Tokyo, 1957.

Ohkawa, K., and Rosovsky, H. "Recent Japanese Growth in Historical Perspective." *American Economic Review*. May 1963.

Ohkita, S. *Shotoku Baizo Keikaku No Kaisetsu* [Interpretation of the income-doubling plan). Tokyo, 1960.

Ohuchi, H., et al. *Nihon Keizai Wa Do Naruka?* [What will become of the Japanese economy?] (Iwanami symposium). Tokyo, 1966.

Organization for Economic Co-operation and Development (OECD). *Economic Surveys: Japan*. Tokyo, 1964 and 1969.

Oriental Economist. *Japan Economic Yearbook*. Tokyo, 1969.

Ozaki, R. S. "Japan's 'Price-Doubling' Plan?." *Asian Survey*. October 1965.

Reischauer, E. O. "Japan Is One of the Biggest Countries in the World." *New York Times Magazine*. October 16, 1966.

Rosovsky, H. "Capital Formation in Pre-War Japan: Current Findings and Future Problems." In *The Economic Development of China and Japan*, edited by C. D. Cowan. London, 1964.

Shibata, T., et al. *Sumiyoi Nihon: Kokumin Seikatsu No Shindan* [Toward a livable Japan: a diagnosis of national living]. Tokyo, 1964.

Shinohara, M. *Kodo Seicho No Himitsu* [The secret of accelerated growth]. Tokyo, 1961.

Shimomura, O. "Seicho Seisaku No Kihon Mondai" [Basic problems of growth policy]. *Riron Keizai Gaku* [Economic Studies Quarterly]. March 1961.

_____. *Nihon Keizai Seicho Ron* [A theory of Japanese economic growth]. Tokyo, 1962.

_____. *Growth and Cycles in the Japanese Economy*. Tokyo, 1962.

_____. "Economic Development and Foreign Trade in Pre-War Japan." In *The Economic Development of China and Japan*, edited by C. D. Cowan. London, 1964.

Tachi, R., et al. *Nihon No Bukka Mondai* [Japan's Price Problems]. Tokyo, 1964.

Taeuber, Irene B. "Population Growth and Economic Development in Japan." *Journal of Economic History*. Fall 1951.

Takeuchi, K. "Some Thoughts on the Economic Problems of Contemporary Japan." *Japan Studies* (English-language publication of Kokusai Nohon Kenkyusho). Vol. 1 (1965).

Tsuru, S., "Business Cycles in Post-War Japan." In *The Business Cycle in the Post-War World*, edited by E. Lundberg. London, 1955.

_____. *Essays on Japanese Economy*. Tokyo, 1958.

_____. "Shotoku Baizo Wa Hatashite Kano Ka?" [Will income-doubling ever be possible?]. *Asahi Jyanaru* [Asahi Journal]. July 19, 1959.

_____. "Growth and Stability in the Postwar Japanese Economy." *American Economic Review*. May 1961.

United States-Japan Trade Council. *The Dollar and the Yen*. Washington, D.C., 1965.

_____. *Protectionism in Disguise*. Washington, D.C., 1966.

_____. *United States Trade with Japan: 1960–64*. Washington, D.C., 1966.

Yamada, I. "The Interindustry Analysis of the Japanese Economy." in *Theory and Application of Interindustry Analysis*. Tokyo, 1961.

Yoshino, T., ed. *Keizai Seicho To Bukka Mondai* [Economic growth and price problems]. Tokyo, 1962.

INDEX

145